Mega-Fun
Map Skills
GRADES 2-3

Catherine M. Tamblyn

SCHOLASTIC
PROFESSIONAL **B**OOKS

NEW YORK • TORONTO • LONDON • AUCKLAND • SYDNEY
MEXICO CITY • NEW DELHI • HONG KONG

DEDICATION

To my family, and to extended family member, Betty:
I thank all of you for your support and the most precious gift of time.

Cover design by Pamela Simmons
Cover photography by Donnelly Marks
Interior design by Solutions by Design, Inc.
Interior illustration by James Graham Hale

ISBN 0-590-18799-6

Contents

Introduction

Every day our young children form a greater connection to the world around them through technology and the media. Coupled with this exposure, they are bombarded with names of places as well as geographical terms for places. Without a strong foundation in place geography, organizing such information can be an overwhelming task. The purpose of this book is to provide activities which will build a solid understanding of globes and maps to help children better understand the world and their place in it.

This book is divided into two parts, **Spin the Globe** and **Unfold the Map,** and includes 37 reproducible pages of maps and cutouts you can use on globes and maps. You'll also find four Sticker Maps and four sheets of reusable stickers bound in the book.

The activities in **Part One: Spin the Globe** give children an opportunity to actively explore the different features of your classroom globe, including the North and South Poles, the equator, and the many symbols used to represent items such as landforms and bodies of water, political divisions, and cities. As children use the globe, they will learn to identify the seven continents, four oceans, and four hemispheres. In addition, they will be able to use the North Pole as a means to locate places using cardinal directions.

The activities in **Part Two: Unfold the Map** help children examine the many features of maps, including title boxes, map keys, and map symbols, and teach children to distinguish between a model and map. The activities also give children the opportunity to use and make a variety of maps. The reproducible maps and cutouts are designed to be used in many different ways. Children can also assemble their maps into their own atlases, which can also serve as geography portfolios.

Both parts contain concepts and skills appropriate for second and third grade classrooms. In each section you'll find activities to teach geography concepts and skills using different tools, including your classroom globe and cutout reproducibles, reproducible maps, or one of the four Sticker Maps and reusable stickers. Activity Options listed after each activity extend the main activity or suggest related activities for exploration, practice, and discovery. Globe & Map Connections, identified by a small globe, allow children to transfer their newly acquired knowledge of globes to maps or vice-versa.

Since models are easier for young children to visualize, you may prefer to cover Part One in its entirety before exploring the maps in Part Two. If you choose to cover the material simultaneously, be sure children are comfortable with the overhead perspective. It is an essential first step in seeing a map as a special kind of picture of a place.

Have fun as you circle the globe and travel the world through maps.

4

Spin the Globe

A Global View

Globes provide the truest possible view of the whole Earth. They duplicate the shape of Earth; all distances, directions, sizes and shapes are true to scale. Globes differ in their depth of content; use of symbols, color and texture; and style. The following activities will help young geographers explore the common features of globes and discover the importance and advantages of their use.

On the Globe

What's a Globe?

A globe is a three-dimensional model of Earth. A model is a small copy of something. Your classroom globe is 30–40 million times smaller than Earth. Globes are useful as they allow us to easily view the land and water on Earth in their true size and form. Introduce globes to your class by displaying photographs of Earth in space next to your classroom globe. Compare and trace the contour of the land shown in the aerial photograph with that on the globe. Label your classroom globe with the term "Globe" from Globe Cutouts (Reproducible 1, page 26).

ACTIVITY OPTIONS

➤ Generate a list of words that describe a globe such as round, a sphere, a model, a copy of Earth, our world, or planet.

➤ To further clarify the concept of models, compare and contrast real objects with their smaller-sized copies, such as a chair and a dollhouse chair, a car and a toy car, or a photograph of real animal and a stuffed animal.

- Speculate as to how aerial views of Earth are taken.

- Discover how different globes represent land, water, and ice.

- Explain to children that some globes are positioned at an angle because Earth's axis always points towards the North Star. During the 24–hour period Earth is making its revolution around the sun, the North Pole always points to the North Star.

- Demonstrate how Earth rotates on its axis in a counterclockwise direction, from east to west.

GLOBE & MAP CONNECTIONS

- Maps are flat drawings of places. To show our round Earth on flat paper, land and bodies of water must be artificially flattened, cut, and stretched. To illustrate this concept, ask children to imagine a map of the world on the skin of an orange. Remove the skin in one big piece and push it flat on a table. That's what map makers do!

- When Earth is shown on paper, land and bodies of water become distorted. The worst distortion appears at the top and bottom of the world. For example, on some world maps, Greenland appears larger than South America. Point out examples of distortion to demonstrate that globes are a more accurate tool when the true size and form of land and water are in question.

Continents & Oceans

Globes show that Earth is made up of land and water—specifically, seven continents and four oceans. Explain to children that a continent is a large body of land.

Locate and trace the outlines of North America, South America, Antarctica, Europe, Africa, Asia, and Australia on your globe. Then use the Globe Cutouts (Reproducible 2, page 27) to label and number the continents, taping the cutouts to the globe. Next, explain that an ocean is a large body of salt water. Locate the Atlantic, Pacific, Indian, and Arctic oceans on your globe and use the Globe Cutouts to number and label them.

ACTIVITY OPTIONS

- Use the "We Live Here" Globe Cutout to mark your continent on the globe.

- Identify the oceans and other bodies of water that border your continent.

- Note the colors used to show continents and oceans on the globe.

- Compare sizes of the continents and oceans. The numbers on the cutouts indicate size from largest to smallest.

- Label the Continent Cutouts (Reproducibles 3–5, pages 28–30) using your globe as a reference. Then paste the cutouts on a round balloon to make a model of Earth.

GLOBE & MAP  CONNECTIONS

- Match continent labels from Globe Cutouts (Reproducible 2, page 27) with Continent Cutouts (Reproducibles 3–5, pages 28–30). Paste the continents in size order on drawing paper.

- Compare and contrast the contour of the land on your globe to land on the North America Map (Reproducible 32, page 57), the hemisphere maps (Reproducibles 33–36, pages 58–61), the World Map (Reproducible 37, page 62) or Sticker Map 4.

- Using your globe as a reference, label continents and oceans on Sticker Map 4 with the stickers from Sticker Sheet 3. Ask children: Which oceans border North America? (Atlantic, Pacific, Arctic) Which ocean does not border Antarctica? (Arctic) Which continents do not border any other continents? (Australia, Antarctica)

- Choose color symbols to identify the continents on the hemisphere maps (Reproducibles 33–36, pages 58–61). Create map keys to accompany the maps.

- Add a compass rose or directional arrows (Reproducible 6, page 31) to any of the maps. Locate continents and oceans using cardinal directions.

Literature Link

Amelia's Fantastic Flight by Rose Bursik (Henry Holt and Company, 1992). Amelia's flight takes her to fourteen countries located on six continents. Trace her flight from city to city on your classroom globe. The trip can also be plotted on Sticker Map 4 using the planes and arrows from Sticker Sheet 2. Ask students: Which continent was not visited? (Antarctica) On which continent did Amelia visit the most countries? (Asia)

Ends of the Earth

The "ends of the earth" are known as the poles. The northernmost place on Earth is the North Pole. The South Pole is the southernmost place. The poles are the coldest places on Earth. Young geographers may be surprised to hear that the South Pole is one of the coldest places on Earth. This may be due to the fact that for those of us who reside in the United States, areas to the south are often recognized as being warmer, while areas to the north are thought of as being cooler.

Locate the poles on your classroom globe and label the North Pole with the polar bear and the South Pole with the penguin from the Globe Cutouts (Reproducible 1, page 26).

GLOBE & MAP CONNECTION

- Using your classroom globe as a reference, locate and label the poles on the Western Hemisphere and Eastern Hemisphere Maps (Reproducibles 33–34, pages 58–59). Locate and label the North Pole on the Northern Hemisphere Map (Reproducible 35, page 60) and the South Pole on the Southern Hemisphere Map (Reproducible 36, page 61). Note that on these two maps, the poles are marked with a + symbol. Using the completed maps, ask children: Which continent is located at the South Pole? (Antarctica) In which hemisphere is the North Pole not shown? (Southern Hemisphere) In which ocean is the North Pole located? (Arctic)

Circle the Equator

The equator is an imaginary line around the middle of Earth. It lies halfway between the poles. The equator is 25,000 miles long. It divides Earth into two equal sections, the Northern Hemisphere and the Southern Hemisphere. Label your classroom globe using the equator arrow from the Globe Cutout (Reproducible 1, page 26). Explain that areas near the equator are the hottest places on Earth. Demonstrate that as one travels away from the equator toward either pole, temperatures gradually change from hot to frigid.

ACTIVITY OPTIONS

➤ Play the game Hot and Cold. Children tell if you are burning hot, warm, cool, cold, or freezing, as you move a toy boat to and from the equator.

➤ Ask children to describe the location of the boat relative to the equator using the terms *above* and *below* or the cardinal directions *north* and *south*.

➤ Think of a continent. Children determine which one by asking questions containing relative terms or cardinal directions.

➤ Ask children to name the continents located on the equator. (South America, Africa, Asia)

GLOBE & MAP  CONNECTIONS

➤ Using your classroom globe as reference, locate and label the equator on the World Map (Reproducible 37, page 62) or on Sticker Map 4 using the equator arrow from Sticker Sheet 3. Have children describe the continents and oceans relative to the equator using the terms *above, north, below, south*, and *on*.

➤ Locate and label the equator on the hemisphere maps (Reproducibles 33–36, pages 58–61). Ask: On which two maps is the equator shown as a complete circle? (Northern Hemisphere, Southern Hemisphere)

Earth's Directions

Direction is the line or course in which something moves, faces or lies. Cardinal directions are Earth's four main directions: north, east, south, and west. Above and below the equator on your classroom globe, tape the large north and south directional arrows (Reproducible 6, page 31). Explain that north is the direction toward the North Pole from any other place on Earth and that south is the direction toward the South Pole. Move your finger on the globe in both directions. Ask children to name the direction and the pole to which you are heading. Affix east and west arrows. Tell children that when you face north, east is always to your right and west is always to your left. Name the location of continents relative to other continents or oceans using cardinal directions.

ACTIVITY OPTIONS

➤ Knowledge of *left* and *right* is a prerequisite for understanding the directions *east* and *west*. To give children practice, draw pictures on the Blank Grid Map (Reproducible 20, page 45). Then use left and right to describe the location of a picture relative to another.

➤ Use a compass to identify true north in your classroom.

➤ Use the midday sun to find north. When children's shadows are straight in front of them, the shadows of their heads are pointing north.

➤ Play Simon Says using relative terms or cardinal directions in your directives.

MEGA-FUN MAP SKILLS
Scholastic Professional Books, 1999

➤ See "Directional Arrows," page 14 for related map activities.

➤ See "Compass Rose," page 14 for activities related to this map symbol.

Four Hemispheres

Explain to children that a globe can be divided in half two ways: as a top half and a bottom half divided by the equator, or as two faces or sides—front and back. Each face or side is called a hemisphere, which means half a sphere. Earth is divided into the Northern Hemisphere and the Southern Hemisphere by the equator. The Northern Hemisphere includes the land and water above the equator. The Southern Hemisphere includes the land and water below the equator. Use the Northern Hemisphere and Southern Hemisphere labels from Globe Cutouts (Reproducible 1, page 26) to identify the hemispheres on your classroom globe.

Earth can also be divided into the Eastern and Western Hemisphere, which are also referred to as faces or sides. The Eastern Hemisphere includes Europe, Africa, Australia, Asia and Antarctica as well as all four oceans. The Western Hemisphere includes North America, South America, and Antarctica and the Atlantic, Pacific, and Arctic oceans.

Use your classroom globe to demonstrate that a person can only see one half of a globe or sphere at any one time. If children have trouble noting this concept on a "busy" globe, use two oranges as models. On one orange, place two toothpicks at either end to represent the poles and draw a circle around the middle to represent the equator. Have children examine the top and bottom of the orange and relate the halves to the Northern and Southern hemispheres. On the second orange, place two toothpicks at either end to represent the poles. Mark an X on one face of the other orange and display it. Point out that the other face or hemisphere cannot be seen while they view the X. Relate this model to the Eastern and Western Hemispheres on your globe.

ACTIVITY OPTIONS

➤ Ask the class to locate and name the two hemispheres in which you reside.

➤ Ask children to locate two continents that are completely within the Southern Hemisphere and two that are completely within the Northern Hemisphere. (Australia, Antarctica, North America, Europe)

GLOBE & MAP CONNECTIONS

➤ Using your classroom globe as a reference, locate and label the Northern and Southern Hemispheres on the World Map (Reproducible 37, page 62). Label the hemispheres on Sticker Map 4 with the labels from Sticker Sheet 3.

➤ Label the continents and oceans on the hemisphere maps (Reproducibles 33–36, pages 58–61). Use the completed maps to name continents and oceans that are located in each of the hemispheres.

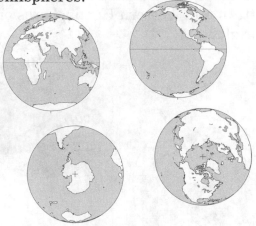

Literature Link

Away From Home by Anita Lobel (Greenwillow Books, 1994) Tour some of the world's cities from A to Z. Start with A and locate them on your classroom globe. It's an ABC journey!

Globe Graphics

Globes vary in their use of symbols. Symbols are lines, shapes, colors, or pictures that stand for real places or things. Examine your classroom globe to find the color symbols that represent types of land, water, and ice. Distinguish between the different symbols used for cities: ⊙ City, ★ Capital City and ✪ National Capital. Identify lines that represent rivers and those that form boundaries between places.

GLOBE & MAP CONNECTIONS

➤ To relate these and other symbols to maps, see "Super Symbols," page 12.

➤ Also see "Political Maps," page 21.

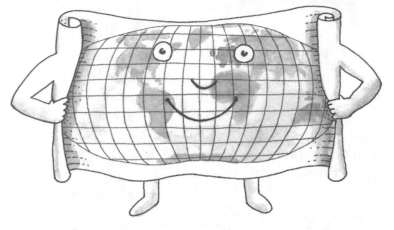

PART TWO

Unfold the Map

Map Talk

Maps are geographic pictures of places that allow us to focus on the characteristics of a place and view an abundance of details in one glance. Maps have a language all their own, which includes labels, numbers, colors, symbols, and small pictures. The following activities will help young geographers learn the language of maps by examining common features found on many different types of maps. As children make and use maps, they will discover the usefulness of maps.

On The Map

What's a Map?

One of the best ways to introduce a map is to compare it to a model. In doing so, children will develop the spatial skills required to visualize a real place from a map. A model is a small copy of a thing or place. Models are three-dimensional. A map is a flat drawing of a place. Examine the similarities and differences with Model and Map (Reproducible 7, page 32).

Ask children: Do the model and map show the same place? (Yes) Which looks the most like a real train yard? Why? (The model, because it is a copy of the Parkerville Train Yard.) Point out that the model shows how the train yard looks from straight ahead and the map shows how it looks from directly overhead. Name items found in the Parkerville Train Yard and ask children to identify the item in both the top and bottom pictures. Children can color or circle matching items as they find them. For example, they might color the pond blue, draw a circle around the freight station, and color the factory red.

ACTIVITY OPTIONS

➤ Have children study a three-dimensional item such as a desk, a chair, a stuffed animal, or a book from eye level (straight ahead) and from directly overhead. Ask children to describe or sketch how the things appear from both perspectives.

➤ Challenge children to create maps of simple models built with clay.

GLOBE & MAP CONNECTION

➤ Discuss the advantages and disadvantages of using models, globes, and maps for finding information. (Models and globes are more accurate but are bulky to carry around. Maps are not as accurate but are more portable. Maps show places in greater detail.)

Title Boxes & Map Keys

To fully understand maps, children need to become familiar with map titles and map keys. Every map contains a title, which is located in a title box. Much like a book's title, a map's title tells what the map is about. Map keys further unlock the meaning of a map as they tell what each color or picture symbol stands for. Without map keys, people would interpret maps differently. Children can play map detective as they look for the map titles and map keys on the reproducible maps and the Sticker Maps. Encourage them to first look for the title box containing the map's title and then study the key for clues to the map's contents and purpose. Use the title box and map key arrows

from Sticker Sheet 1 to identify these features on Sticker Maps 1, 3, and 4.

ACTIVITY OPTIONS

➤ Cut out the Parkerville Train Yard Map and paste it on paper. Prepare a key for the map using the blank map key (Reproducible 8, page 33).

➤ Make your own maps and map keys using the Map Keys (Reproducible 8, page 33) and Map Symbols (Reproducibles 9–10, pages 34–35).

Super Symbols

Symbols on a map stand for real places and things. Symbols can be pictures, shapes, colors, or lines. Many maps for the primary grades contain picture symbols that are three-dimensional, which can make it difficult for young geographers to grasp the concept that maps are flat representations of places. To avoid any confusion, map symbols in this book are flat, as they would appear from directly above, or they are presented in panels resembling signs. The following activities introduce map symbols.

Picture Symbols

Most maps for children show representations of things or places through the use of picture symbols or shapes. A picture symbol is a drawing or shape that stands for a real thing. Picture symbols on maps are not standardized; however, people have come to recognize some as common representations of places and things. Many of these symbols appear on road signs in our communities or along highways. The same picture symbol can represent different things on different maps. Examine Map Symbols (Reproducibles 9–10, pages 34–35) to identify places or things each symbol could represent. For example, the bicycle symbol could represent a bicycle shop or a bicycle path on a map. Challenge children to create a map key using the picture symbols and the blank map key (Reproducible 8, page 33).

Color Symbols

A color symbol is a color that stands for a real thing. Like picture symbols, the same color symbol might stand for different things on a variety of maps. The color green, for example, might represent a park on one map and stand for land on another. Physical maps generally use a more standard palette of color symbols, such as pale green to represent plains, dark green to represent hills, tan to represent deserts, and browns, oranges and reds to represent mountains. The World Map (Reproducible 37, page 62) can be used to apply the basic color symbols: green for land and blue for water. Have children prepare the map key and then color the map accordingly.

➤ The shaded and unshaded geometric shapes from the Map Symbols (Reproducibles 9–10, pages 34–35) can function as color and/or picture symbols on children's maps. Use squares for single-family homes, circles for places of business, rectangles for apartment buildings, diamonds for mobile homes, and so on.

➤ Use the completed map in "Create Your Own Atlas," p. 25.

Lines

Lines are symbols used to designate boundaries, borders, rivers, and roads on maps. They are also used to show routes. A route is the course used for traveling from one place to another. Use the Clear Lake Map (Reproducible 11, page 36) to trace the route of a park ranger. Ask children: Where did the ranger start and end her route? (Information) Which campsite did she visit first? (A) What trail did the ranger cross? (The hiking trail) How many times did she cross it? (4 times) Did she go on the horse trail? (No) Did she visit every picnic site? (Yes)

ACTIVITY OPTIONS

➤ Expand the Clear Lake Map by having children draw additional route lines and adding appropriate Map Symbols (Reproducibles 9–10, pages 34–35). Use the blank map key (Reproducible 8, page 33) for the new map key.

➤ Outline different routes for children to follow on Sticker Map 1. Use the route arrows and directional arrows from Sticker Sheet 2 to represent different routes and directions.

➤ Incorporate route line symbols on any reproducible maps for children to read and interpret.

Directional Arrows

Maps for young children often include arrows that indicate cardinal directions. These arrows show the orientation of the map and help determine the location of places on a map. Remind children that north is not always at the top of every map. Use Earth's Directions Map (Reproducible 12, page 37) to demonstrate opposite directions on Earth. Have children cut out all of the elements on the page. Then they should glue the earth on a sheet of paper and affix the four directional arrows in the appropriate spot, beginning with "north." Finally, at the bottom of the page, they should glue the child cutout, with "right" and "left" labels on either side. Point out that when you face north, south is directly behind you, east is to your right, and west is to your left.

ACTIVITY OPTIONS

➢ Explain that east is the direction in which the morning sun appears and west is the direction of the sunset.

➢ Add directional arrows from Sticker Sheet 1 to Sticker Maps 1–4.

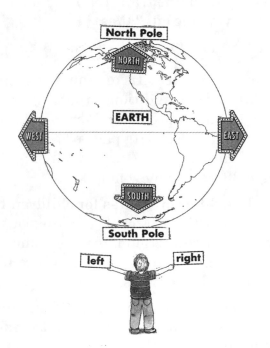

Compass Rose

Many primary level maps contain a simple compass rose which indicates the four cardinal directions. More complex compass roses show intermediate directions. Unlike directional arrows, a compass rose indicates direction using only the letters *N, E, S,* and *W.* Introduce the Compass Rose (Reproducible 13, p. 38) as a drawing on a map that shows cardinal directions. Share what the letters on each point stand for. Then have children cut out the labels on the bottom of the page and paste them to the inner points of the compass rose to identify the four main directions and the intermediate directions northeast, southeast, northwest, and southwest.

ACTIVITY OPTIONS

➢ Add the compass rose to any oversized map or use it for cover art for "Create Your Own Atlas," page 25.

➢ Demonstrate that a real compass shows the true direction in space. Show children how the compass needle points to north in your classroom. Using the compass for reference, help children affix their compass roses to their desks or to post direction labels in your classroom.

➢ Add a compass rose (Reproducible 6, page 31) to any reproducible map.

➢ Add a compass rose from Sticker Sheet 1 to Sticker Maps 1–4.

➢ Identify north arrows on maps as other indicators of direction. A north arrow cutout appears on Directional Arrows (Reproducible 6, page 31.)

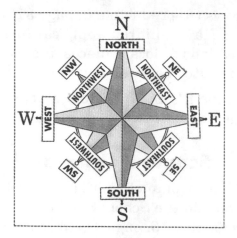

Insets

Insets are small geographic representations that are set within boxes on a larger map. Identify this feature on Sticker Map 3 using the inset map arrows from Sticker Sheet 1. Name the contents of each inset map. Suggest reasons why insets are necessary, such as for the purpose of space. Similar insets appear on the United States Maps (Reproducibles 30–31, pages 55–56).

Locators

Locators are small maps included on a larger, main map. A locator shows where the area in the main map is located. Identify this feature on Sticker Map 3 using the locator map arrow from Sticker Sheet 1. The same locator map appears on the United States Maps (Reproducibles 30–31, pages 55–56) and on the North America Map (Reproducible 32, page 57).

GLOBE & MAP CONNECTION

➤ Hunt for locators on maps in magazines or newspapers and identify the regions shown on your classroom globe.

A Menu of Maps

There are many kinds of maps. Each provides a different type of information. Activities for exploring a variety of maps are included in this section.

Floor Plans

A floor plan is a drawing of the surface of a room or building which shows the location of windows and doors. Floor plans vary in detail. Some show empty rooms, while others show the placement of furniture, appliances, and other structures within these rooms. In floor plans, the view is generally from directly overhead.

Play Land Floor Plan

Use the Play Land Floor Plan (Reproducible 14, page 39) to identify the characteristics of a floor plan. Remind children that the view of the ship, log cabin, and covered wagon is from directly overhead. Point out that the doors on this map are indicated by a solid line. Invite children to draw picture symbols for each room. For example, a fish for the Aquarium, party hats or balloons for the Party Rooms, and a computer for the Computer Room.

ACTIVITY OPTIONS

➤ Add directional arrows or a compass rose (Reproducible 6, page 31) to the map. Locate rooms or identify the number of windows or doors on each side of the building using cardinal directions.

➤ Reinforce the meaning of relative

terms by having children locate rooms and other features in the building using terms such as *next to, near, far from, outside,* and *to the right/left.*

➤ Ask children to draw a route on the map that connects five places they would visit at Play Land.

Mall Floor Plan

This open-ended map (Reproducibles 17–18, pages 42–43) allows children to demonstrate their knowledge of space and use of space in a creative way. Each child can plan his or her own mall or the class can collectively prepare one floor plan. To create the floor plan, paste Reproducible 17 and Reproducible 18 together. Review the floor plan with children, identifying each single line as a doorway and labeling each outer doorway as an exit. Note the different sizes of spaces on the map and discuss what type of store might occupy each space. Generate a list of things that could be found in the open area such as tables and chairs, benches, trees, and so on. Children can then cut and paste the Map Symbols (Reproducibles 9–10, pages 34–35) to represent stores in the mall. Children can add a blank map key (Reproducible 8, page 33) and then use the symbols to create a map key for their mall.

ACTIVITY OPTIONS

➤ Use the completed map to locate shops using relative terms and to establish routes from one location to another.

➤ Compare children's floor plans, pointing out differences and similarities in how children set up their malls and how they used different symbols. Discuss why children selected particular locations for each store.

➤ Add a compass rose or directional arrows (Reproducible 6, page 31) to the map. Have children apply cardinal directions to locate places and establish routes between locations.

➤ Use the Blank Map (Reproducible 29, page 54) to draw a floor plan.

School Floor Plan

Draw a floor plan of your school and have children add the School Symbols (Reproducible 16, page 41) to represent different rooms in your school.

ACTIVITY OPTIONS

➤ Let children draw their own school floor plans and use the School Symbols to label them. Children can cut and paste the School Symbols (Reproducible 16, page 41) to the floor plan.

➤ Use the School Floor Plan in "Create Your Own Atlas," page 25.

Classroom Floor Plan

Use the Classroom Cutouts (Reproducible 15, page 40) and a large sheet of construction paper to create a floor plan of your classroom. Use the completed floor plan to discuss the relative location of items and to establish routes from one location to another.

➤ Include your Classroom Floor Plan in "Create Your Own Atlas," page 25.

Grid Maps

A grid map is divided by lines that run from side to side and from top to bottom. Grid maps allow us to locate places or things using absolute, or exact location.

Sticker Map 2: Grid Map

Introduce grid maps with Sticker Map 2. Point out that the crossing lines form rows of squares. Label above the rows that run from side to side with numbers 1 to 6 from Sticker Sheet 4. Label next to those that run from top to bottom with letters A to D from Sticker Sheet 4. Demonstrate how to use the grid map. Run one finger down the row of squares that is labeled with the number 5 and run another finger across the row of squares that is labeled with the letter C. Explain that the square where the two rows meet is C5. Label the square with the appropriate sticker from Sticker Sheet 4. Continue to label each of the squares on the grid map with the appropriate stickers. Once children understand the grid map, invite them to fill in the remaining squares with the appropriate stickers.

ACTIVITY OPTIONS

➤ Place any of the map symbols from Sticker Sheet 4 in random squares. Ask children to name the location of each symbol with a number and letter.

➤ Add map symbols to the grid map and attach a card naming five or more number and letter labels. Have children, working in small groups, identify and make a list of items in each square.

➤ Place letters cards labeled A to D in one box and number cards labeled from 1 to 6 in another box. Place symbol stickers in each box on the grid map. Have children choose one card from each box and name the item in that location.

➤ For more practice with grid maps, use masking tape to make a large grid map on the floor. Place a child in each square. Ask questions such as: Who is above/north of Andrew? What is that square's label/location?

➤ Add directional arrows or a compass rose from Sticker Sheet 1 to the grid map and ask children to locate items relative to other items using cardinal directions.

Ocean Floor Grid Map

Children can hunt for sunken treasure with the Ocean Floor Grid Map (Reproducible 19, page 44). Name grid coordinates and have children color the items that they find in that box. For example, children might color the coins in C6 gold and the starfish in A1 pink. Then have children take an inventory of items they find on the ocean floor and list each item's letter and number coordinate to make a location directory for the map.

Blank Grid Map

Use the Blank Grid Map (Reproducible 20, page 45) and the Garden Greens Cutouts (Reproducible 21, page 46) to make a Garden Greens grid map. Have children begin by labeling the horizontal rows with Seed Packets A to D and the vertical rows with Watering Cans 1 to 6. Then children can fill in their gardens with any of the cutouts they choose. Finally, children can make a list of the items in their garden by naming each item's location.

ACTIVITY OPTIONS

➤ Children can make a community grid map using the Map Symbols (Reproducibles 9–10, pages 34–35).

➤ Make a grid map picture puzzle. Give each child two copies of the Blank Grid Map. Have children label each square on two grid maps with the appropriate number and letter. Then have them draw a picture or design on the back of one grid map; and then cut the squares apart. Partners recreate the puzzle, picture side up, on the uncut grid map.

➤ Play a game of Directions with the map. Have children add directional arrows or a compass rose (Reproducible 6, page 31) to the grid map. To begin children locate a "start" square according to your directions. Then have children move around the grid according to your directions. For example: Move north two squares. Color that square blue. Move east three squares. Color that square red.

➤ Play Bingo with the blank grid map. Have children randomly fill the squares with vocabulary words. Then, as you call out words, children place markers on the words until someone completes a row. Players must name each square's coordinates to win.

➤ Name labels and have children add items to their grid maps one-by-one.

➤ Use the map in conjunction with Sticker Map 2. Both maps may be positioned horizontally and vertically.

Street Maps

Street or road maps help guide travelers from one place to another. They can show major highways, roadways, country lanes, dirt roads, even roads under construction!

Sticker Map 1: Newtown's Streets

Begin by generating a list of different names for streets, such as *road, highway, parkway, lane, thruway, avenue, boulevard, route, interstate,* and so on. Display Sticker Map 1 and identify the different types of roads on the map. Locate the bridges, exits, and the construction area. Then use the stickers from Sticker Sheet 2 to label the roads on the map. To make the task easier, you might start by asking children to label First Street, Third Street, and Fourth Street. Then children can fill in the rest of the street names and exit labels.

ACTIVITY OPTIONS

➤ Have children use the map to determine different routes. Ask questions such as: How would you direct someone from Avenue A to the bicycle path on First Street? What is the best way to get from the corner of Avenue A and Fourth Street to the bicycle path on Avenue C? What are alternate routes? Children can use the arrow stickers on Sticker Sheet 2 to show different routes. Make the activity more challenging by adding the one way stickers to different roads.

➤ Children can add to Newtown using the symbols on Sticker Sheet 2 and Sticker Sheet 4. The circles, squares, and rectangles on Sticker Sheet 2 can represent houses, apartments, or stores. Children can also use any of the map symbols from Sticker Sheet 4.

MEGA-FUN MAP SKILLS
Scholastic Professional Books, 1999

> Add directional arrows or a compass rose from Sticker Sheet 1. Ask children to name locations and describe routes using cardinal directions.

Urban Area Map

Hand out copies of the Urban Area Map (Reproducibles 22–23, pages 47–48). Children can assemble the map by pasting the reproducibles together along First Street. Remind children of the terms *urban area, community,* and *city.* Explain that a community is a place that is made up of many different neighborhoods; a city is a large community with many people; and an urban area is a city and the places around it. Read the names of the streets and note their pattern.

ACTIVITY OPTIONS

> Have children use the map to plan routes. Give directions for getting from one street to another across the map and ask children to trace or draw the route. Name two streets and ask children to identify possible routes to get from one to the other.

> Invite children to use the Map Symbols (Reproducibles 9–10, pages 34–35) to map out a city. Children can cut out and paste symbols to the map. Remind children to think about what types of businesses they would find in an urban area. Have children add a blank map key (Reproducible 8, page 33) the left side of the map to identify the symbols.

> Compare children's maps to note the variety of places shown. Discuss the reasons for the arrangement of places. Name and trace routes from one location to another.

> Ask children to add directional arrows or a compass rose (Reproducible 6, page 31) to their maps and then use cardinal

directions to describe and locate places on the map.

> Expand the map by attaching the Suburban Community Map (Reproducible 24, page 49) along Fourth Street, and the Rural Area Map (Reproducible 25, page 50) along Beech Tree Road. Children use the Map Symbols (Reproducible 9–10, pages 34–35) to make a tri-community map. See the Suburban Community Map and Rural Area Map for more activity options.

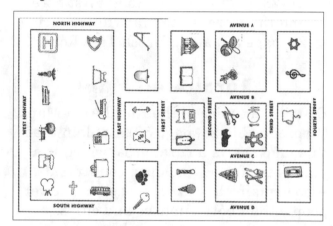

Suburban Community Map

Hand out copies of the Suburban Community Map (Reproducible 24, page 49) to the class. Explain that this map shows some streets in a suburban community and that a *suburb* is a community just outside of a city. Note the names of the roads and discuss how this map is different from the Urban Area Map. Ask children to trace and plan routes from one street to another.

ACTIVITY OPTIONS

> Children can map a suburban community by pasting on appropriate Map Symbols (Reproducibles 9–10, pages 34–35). Then they should add a blank map key (Reproducible 8, page 33) and complete it to identify the meaning of the symbols.

➤ Compare children's maps. Note the variety of places children have included on their maps and discuss the different ways children have set up their maps and discuss the reasons for their placement.

➤ Have children add directional arrows or a compass rose (Reproducible 6, page 31) to the map and then use cardinal directions to describe and locate places.

➤ Expand this map by attaching the Urban Area Maps (Reproducibles 22–23, pages 47–48) along First Street and the Rural Area Map (Reproducible 25, page 50) along Beech Tree Road.

Rural Area Map

Distribute copies of the Rural Area Map (Reproducible 25, page 50). Explain that this map shows a rural area, which is a place with farms and open countryside. Also explain that *rural* areas have fewer people than both suburbs and cities. Compare this map to the Urban Area Map and the Suburban Community Map and discuss the differences. Note the names of the roads and trace them.

ACTIVITY OPTIONS

➤ Discuss with children the types of places they would find in a rural community. Then children can use the map to create a rural community by pasting on appropriate Map Symbols (Reproducibles 9–10, pages 34–35).

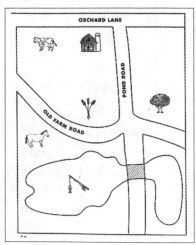

➤ Compare children's maps and note the variety of places shown.

➤ Have children add directional arrows or a compass rose (Reproducible 6, page 31) to the map to describe and locate places using cardinal directions.

➤ Name and trace routes from one location to another. Identify alternate routes.

➤ Attach this map to the Suburban Community Map (Reproducible 24, page 49) along Beech Tree Road.

Transportation Maps

Transportation maps show routes people use to travel from place to place. They often show major roadways, railways, airports and other kinds of transportation all on the same map. Hand out copies of the Transportation Map (Reproducible 26, page 51). Work together to identify the symbols used on the map. Ask questions such as: Which three kinds of transportation stop near the Tinton Falls airport? (railroad, subway, bus) Which communities have ferry stops? (Little Silver, Shrewsbury) On which bus route is Shrewsbury (2) What is the next stop after Red Bank on bus route 1? (Tinton Falls)

ACTIVITY OPTION

➤ Challenge children to create their own Transportation Map on a blank sheet of paper using the Map Symbols (Reproducibles 9–10, pages 34–35) and the Transportation Map Key (Reproducible 8, page 33).

Physical Maps

Physical maps, also known as landform maps, can show vegetation, terrain, elevation of the terrain, and other natural features of places using color symbols, picture symbols, or a combination of both.

20

Land and Water Book

To help children understand some of the features of physical maps, have them complete a Land and Water Book (Reproducibles 27–28, pages 52–53). To make the book, have children cut along the outer rules of both reproducibles and glue the cutouts back-to-back. Then cut out the horizontal page strips and stack them so that the page numbers on the left appear as 1, 3, 5, 7 from the bottom, up. Fold the strips in half and staple them together on the fold. Children create their own color symbols and use references to identify specific bodies of water and landforms in the United States. Have children label the drawing at the back of the book and add individual drawings to pages as desired.

ACTIVITY OPTIONS

➤ Invite children to create landforms and bodies of water using clay, sand, or shaving cream.

➤ Challenge children to create a physical map on a blank sheet of paper, including adding map symbols to their map keys. They can use the Land and Water Map Key (Reproducible 8, page 33).

➤ Add the mountain symbol and map key label from Sticker Sheet 3 to identify Mt. McKinley on Sticker Map 3.

➤ Working together, add landform symbols to the United States Map, (Reproducible 30, page 55) or the World Map (Reproducible 37, page 62).

GLOBE & MAP CONNECTIONS

➤ Compare landform symbols on globes to those on maps.

➤ Use a physical relief globe to help you make a physical map of the United States with the Land and Water Map Key (Reproducible 8, page 33) and the United States Map (Reproducible 30, page 55).

Political Maps

Political maps show cities and the boundaries between places. Boundaries or borders on a map reflect the political divisions agreed upon by communities, counties, states or nations. Some borders follow natural features and others were plotted by surveyors.

Sticker Map 3: United States Map

Post Sticker Map 3 and hand out copies of the United States Map (Reproducible 30, page 55) for children to refer to as you work with the Sticker Map. Identify the United States as a country with 50 states. Explain that a country is a nation and the people who live there. A state is part of a country. Trace the boundaries of the United States and identify the neighboring countries. Trace the boundaries of your state and identify the surrounding states. Add the arrows and labels from Sticker Sheets 1 and 3 to identify countries, bodies of water, your state, and the U.S. capital. Add the National and State Capital stickers to the map key. Name the states and bodies of water shown in the two inset maps.

ACTIVITY OPTIONS

➤ Have children add the flags from Globe Cutouts (Reproducible 2, page 27) to the appropriate countries on their United States Map (Reproducible 30, page 55).

➤ Add directional arrows or a compass rose (Reproducible 6, page 31) to the map to apply cardinal directions in terms of identifying routes.

➤ Ask children to use color and picture symbols to show the Rocky Mountains, the Appalachian Mountains, the Coast Ranges, Mt. McKinley, the Great Plains, the Coastal Plains, and more on their United States Map.

➤ Mark historic sites on Sticker Map 3 with the stickers from Sticker Sheet 3. Explain to children that each sticker represents a historical landmark in the United States. The sites represented include Abe Lincoln's birthplace (Kentucky), the Gateway Arch (Missouri), Mount Vernon (Virginia), the Alamo (Texas), Golden Gate Bridge (California), the Statue of Liberty (New York), and Mount Rushmore (Sout Dakota). Children can also add the historic sites to their United States map using the Map Symbols (Reproducible 10, page 35) and create a map key listing the sites.

➤ Challenge children to write the 2-letter standard abbreviations for each state on the map.

➤ Have children make a stately names map. Explain that they should color only the states that have a person's first name contained within the state's name. Here are some possibilities:

FLO—**Flo**rida
MARY—**Mary**land
TEX—**Tex**as
WES—**Wes**t Virginia
KEN—**Ken**tucky
LOU—**Lou**isiana
DIANA—In**diana**
IDA—**Ida**ho or Flor**ida**
EVA—N**eva**da
LOUIS—**Louis**iana
CAROL—North or South **Carol**ina
VIRGINIA—West **Virginia** or **Virginia**
ANA—Indi**ana**, Mont**ana**, Louisi**ana**

United States: Capital Cities Map

ACTIVITY OPTIONS

➤ Distinguish between the ✪ National Capital and the ★ State Capital symbols on the United States: Capital Cities Map (Reproducible 31, page 56) Explain that a capital city is where the leaders of a state work.

➤ Challenge children to make a capital names map by coloring the states that have a first name contained within the capital city's name. Here are some possibilities:

ANN or ANNA—**Ann**apolis, MD
ART—H**art**ford, CT
GUS—Au**gus**ta, ME
CHARLES—**Charles**ton, WV
SAL—**Sal**em, OR
RICH—**Rich**mond, VA
JACK—**Jack**son, MS
AL—**Al**bany, NY
JUNE—**June**au, AK
TRENT—**Trent**on, NJ
DIANA—In**diana**polis, IN
PIERRE—**Pierre**, SD
FRANK—**Frank**fort, KY
HELEN—**Helen**a, MT
LULU—Hono**lulu**, HI
PAUL—St. **Paul**, MN
MADISON—**Madison**, WI
AUSTIN—**Austin**, TX
PIA—Olym**pia**, WA
JEFF—**Jeff**erson City, MO

➤ Compare the capital names map to the stately names map. Ask: Which states have a first name included in both their capital city's name and their state name? (Indiana, Maryland, West Virginia, Virginia, Kentucky, Montana)

Literature Link

The Armadillo From Amarillo by Lynne Cherry (Harcourt Brace & Co., 1994). Use a map of Texas or a United States map to plot the adventures of an armadillo as he travels through the cities of Texas and beyond.

World Map

ACTIVITY OPTIONS

➤ Identify land and water on the World Map (Reproducible 37, page 62) using the color symbols green and blue. Complete the map key accordingly. Ask: Which continents are bordered by the Indian Ocean? (Australia, Asia, Africa, Antarctica) Which continents are bordered by the Pacific Ocean? (Australia, North America, South America, Asia, Antarctica)

➤ Label the equator.

➤ Add directional arrows or a compass rose (Reproducible 6, page 31) to the map.

➤ Use the map in conjunction with Sticker Map 4 and Sticker Sheets 1 and 3.

GLOBE & MAP  CONNECTIONS

➤ Use the globe to number the continents and oceans in size order.

➤ Gather clothing and food items from different countries. Locate the countries of origin on your classroom globe and then draw pictures of the items on the appropriate continents on the map.

North America Map

This map (Reproducible 32, page 57) shows North America, which is the third largest continent and covers 9,385,000 sq. miles. It includes Greenland, Canada, the United States, Mexico, Central America, and the West Indies.

ACTIVITY OPTIONS

➤ Name some of the countries that make up North America and use color symbols to identify them on the map and in the key. Locate bordering bodies of water.

➤ Add directional arrows or a compass rose (Reproducible 6, page 31) to the map. Determine the location of countries and oceans relative to the United States.

➤ Use the map in conjunction with Sticker Map 4 and Sticker Sheets 1 and 3.

➤ Label North America on the Western Hemisphere Map (Reproducible 33, page 58) and on the Northern Hemisphere Map (Reproducible 35, page 60).

GLOBE & MAP  CONNECTIONS

➤ Use your classroom globe to identify the land not labeled on the map.

➤ Add flags from Globe Cutouts (Reproducible 2, page 27) to both the globe and map.

Western Hemisphere Map

ACTIVITY OPTIONS

➤ Note that the view of the Western Hemisphere Map (Reproducible 33, page 58) is from a position even with the equator. Locate and label the equator and the poles.

➤ Label continents and oceans using the World Map (Reproducible 37, page 62) as reference. As an alternative, label only the oceans and use different colors to identify the continents. Prepare a map key using the same color symbols. Encourage consistent use of colors on all hemisphere maps.

➤ Compare the four completed hemisphere maps (Reproducibles 33–36, pages 58–61). Name the continents appearing on each.

➤ Compare this map to the Eastern Hemisphere Map (Reproducible 33, page 58) to find which hemisphere has more land. (Eastern)

➤ Add directional arrows or a compass rose (Reproducible 6, page 31) to the map.

Eastern Hemisphere Map

ACTIVITY OPTIONS

➤ Note that the view of the Eastern Hemisphere Map (Reproducible 34, page 59) is from a position even with the equator. Locate and label the equator and the poles.

➤ Label continents and oceans using the World Map (Reproducible 37, page 62) as reference. As an alternative, label only the oceans and use different colors to identify the continents. Use the same colors in the map key. Encourage a consistent use of colors on all hemisphere maps.

➤ Add directional arrows or a compass rose (Reproducible 6, page 31) to the map.

Northern Hemisphere Map

ACTIVITY OPTIONS

➤ Note that the view of the Northern Hemisphere Map (Reproducible 35, page 60) is from above the North Pole. Label the + symbol North Pole and the map's circular band equator.

➤ Label continents and oceans using the World Map (Reproducible 37, page 62) as reference. As an alternative, only label the oceans and use different colors to identify the continents. Use similar colors in the map key. Encourage a consistent use of colors on all hemisphere maps.

Southern Hemisphere Map

ACTIVITY OPTIONS

➤ Note that the view of the Southern Hemisphere Map (Reproducible 36, page 61) is from above the South Pole. Label the + symbol, South Pole, and the map's circular band equator.

➤ Label continents and oceans using the World Map (Reproducible 37, page 62) as reference. As an alternative, label only the oceans and use different colors to identify the continents. Use similar colors in the map key. Encourage a consistent use of colors on all hemisphere maps.

➤ Compare this map to the Northern Hemisphere Map (Reproducible 35, page 60) to find which hemisphere has more water. (Southern)

➤ Compare the four completed hemisphere maps (Reproducibles 33–36, pages 58–61). Ask: In which two hemispheres does Australia appear? (Southern, Eastern) Which map does not show South America? (Eastern Hemisphere)

24

GLOBE & MAP  CONNECTIONS

➢ See "Four Hemispheres," page 9.

➢ Compare the Northern and Southern Hemisphere maps to your globe.

Historical Maps

Historical maps can show a range of data about the past, including location of battlegrounds, communities, routes traveled, or land use. When compared to current maps, historical maps often show tremendous changes. Make your own state history come alive by creating a historical map of your state! Use an overhead projector to show an outline of your state. Project the image onto a sheet of white butcher paper and trace its outline. Decorate with symbols that represent landmarks in your state. You can feature early cities, topographic features, historic sites, and so on.

ACTIVITY OPTIONS

➢ Make a map of your state today for comparison.

➢ Mark the location of historic places on Sticker Map 3, including the Alamo, the Statue of Liberty, and the Golden Gate Bridge, with the stickers from Sticker Sheet 3.

➢ Prepare a map of the first Thirteen States using the United States Map (Reproducible 30, page 55). Color Maine (which was part of Massachusetts), New Hampshire, Massachusetts, New York, Connecticut, New Jersey, Pennsylvania, Delaware, Maryland, Virginia, North Carolina, South Carolina, and Georgia. Paste the colored portion of the map onto a Blank Map (Reproducible 29, page 54).

Literature Link

After reading **Roxboxen** by Alice McLerran (Scholastic Inc., 1991), encourage children to create a historical map of the magical world of Roxaboxen. Children can use clues from the story to plan their map and use found objects such as buttons, yarn, and string to make their maps.

Atlas Maker

Create Your Own Atlas

Children will enjoy making their own atlases featuring maps they have studied and maps they have created. Have children construct an atlas using a solid color two pocket folder with brads. As they complete the maps in this book, children can add them to their atlas. Oversized maps and photographs of children's work can be placed in the folder's pockets. They can use the compass rose they created (Reproducible 13, page 38) for the cover. Be sure children prepare a table of contents for their atlases.

REPRODUCIBLE 1: **Globe Cutouts**

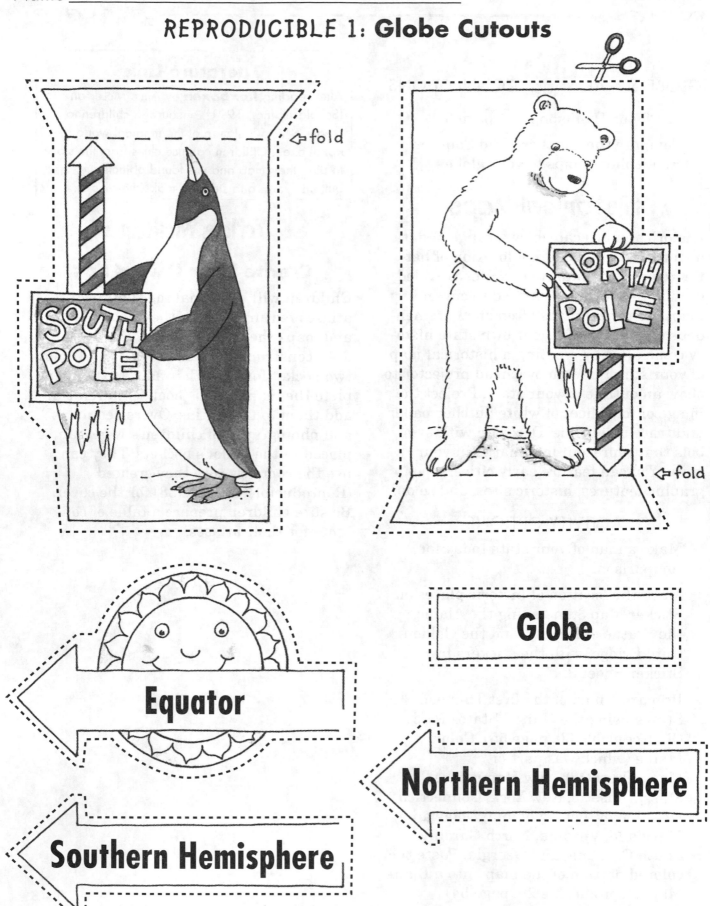

MEGA-FUN MAP SKILLS
Scholastic Professional Books, 1999

Name _____

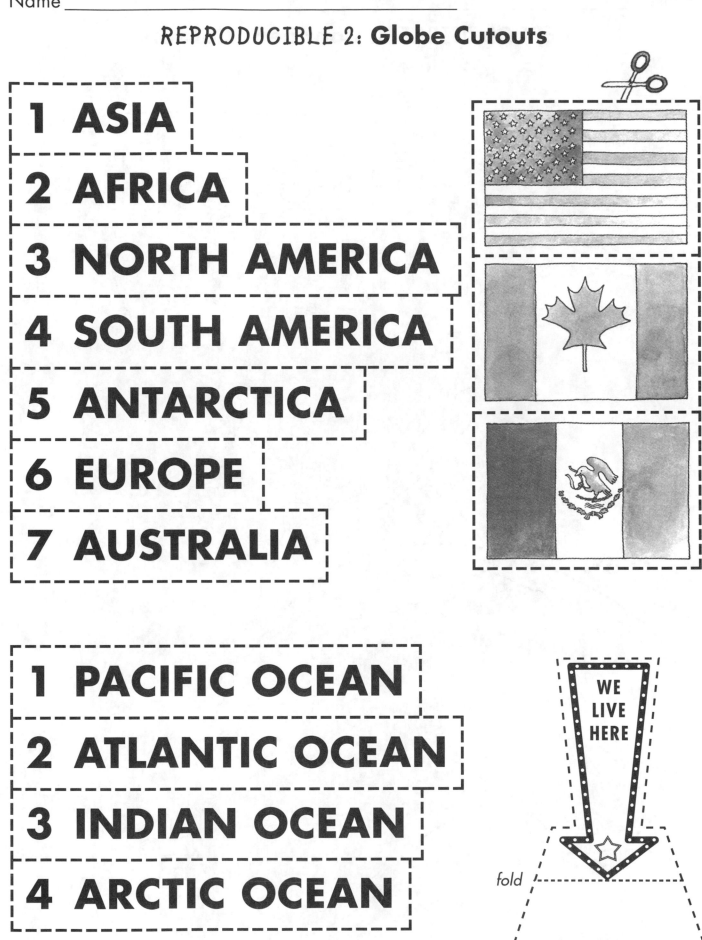

1 ASIA

2 AFRICA

3 NORTH AMERICA

4 SOUTH AMERICA

5 ANTARCTICA

6 EUROPE

7 AUSTRALIA

1 PACIFIC OCEAN

2 ATLANTIC OCEAN

3 INDIAN OCEAN

4 ARCTIC OCEAN

WE LIVE HERE

fold

Name _____

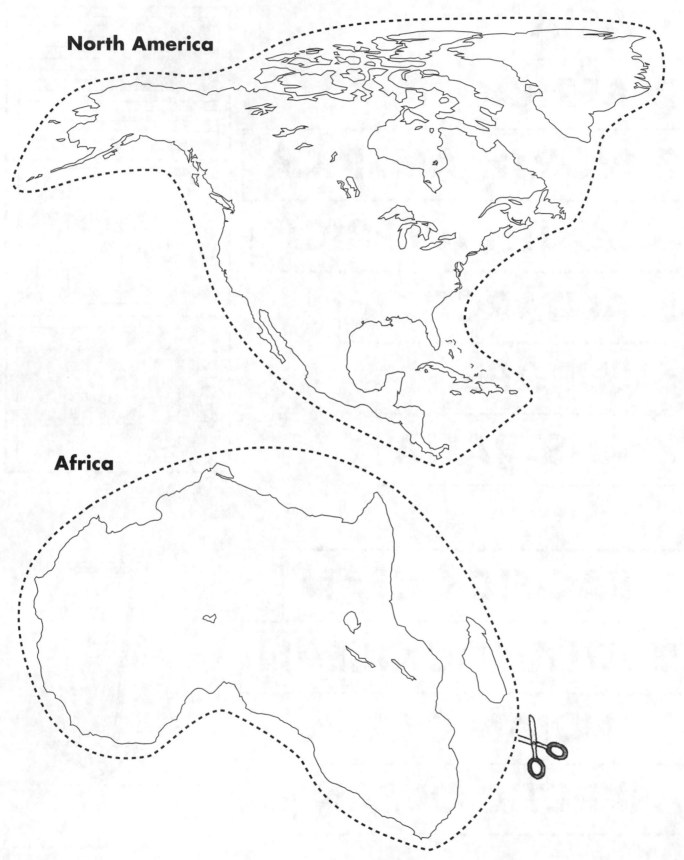

North America

Africa

MEGA-FUN MAP SKILLS
Scholastic Professional Books, 1999

REPRODUCIBLE 4: **Continent Cutouts**

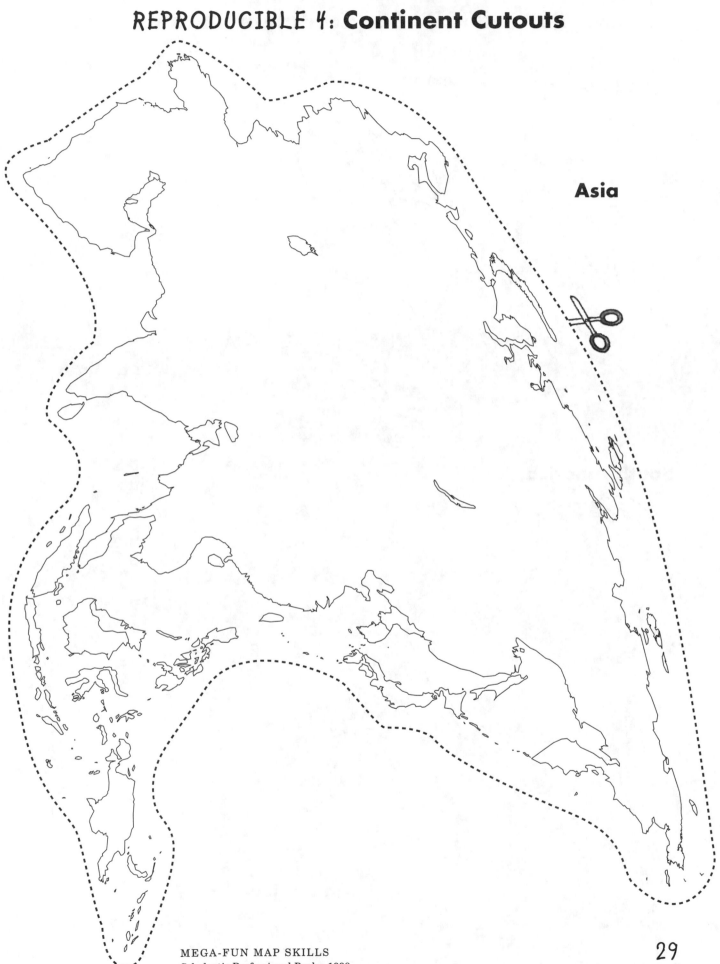

Asia

MEGA-FUN MAP SKILLS
Scholastic Professional Books, 1999

29

Name_____

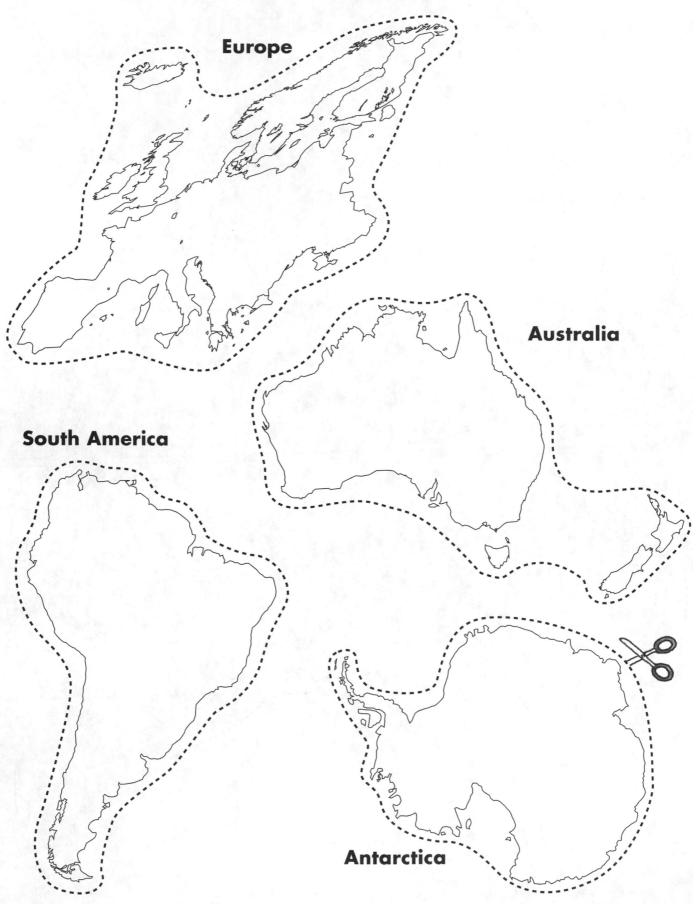

Europe

Australia

South America

Antarctica

MEGA-FUN MAP SKILLS
Scholastic Professional Books, 1999

REPRODUCIBLE 6: **Directional Arrows and Compass Roses**

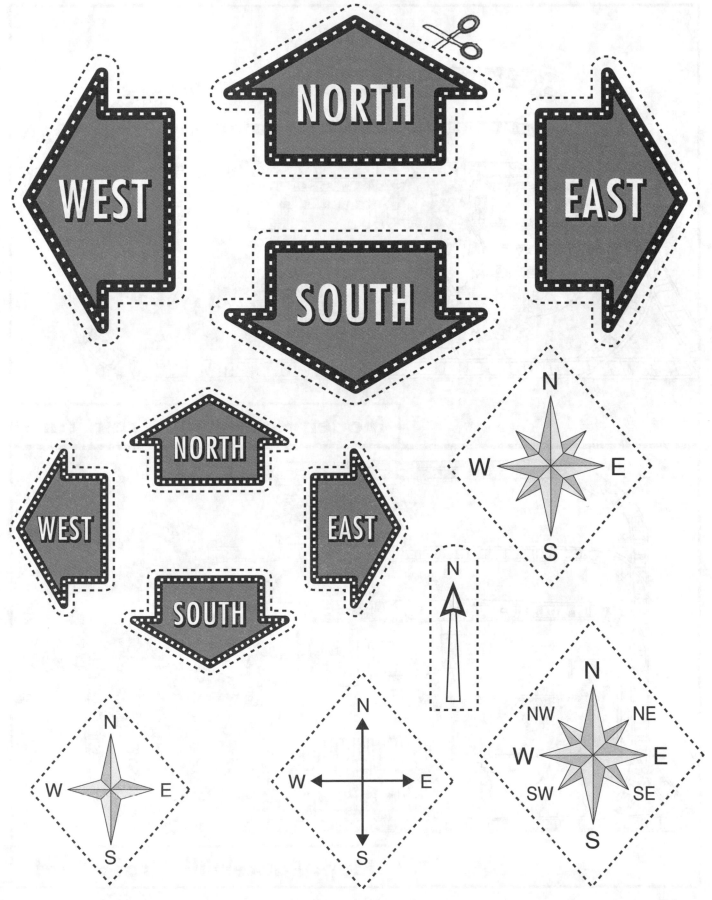

REPRODUCIBLE 7: Model and Map

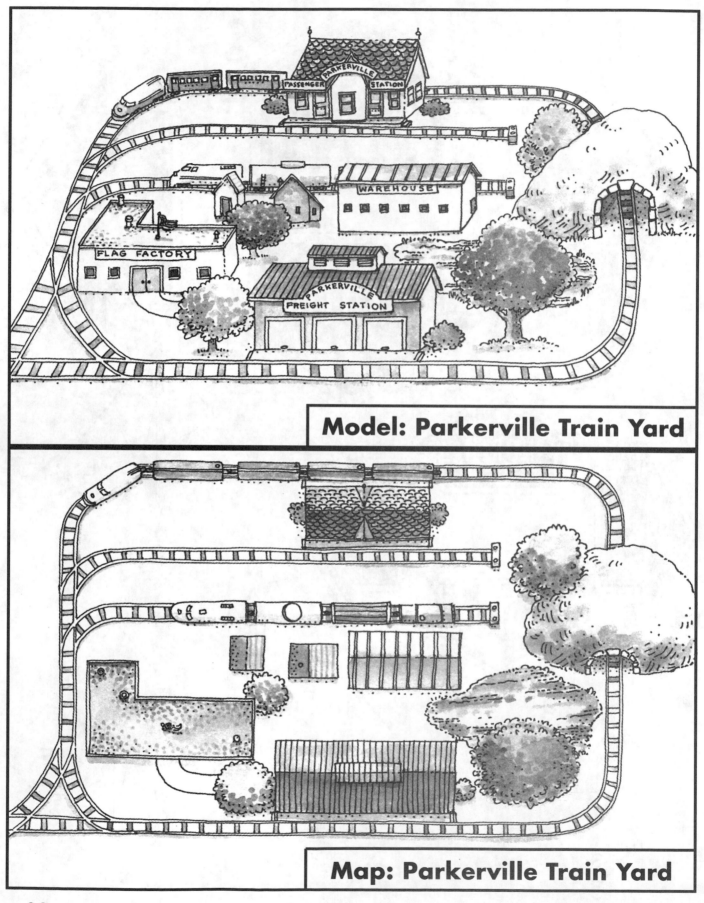

Model: Parkerville Train Yard

Map: Parkerville Train Yard

MEGA-FUN MAP SKILLS
Scholastic Professional Books, 1999

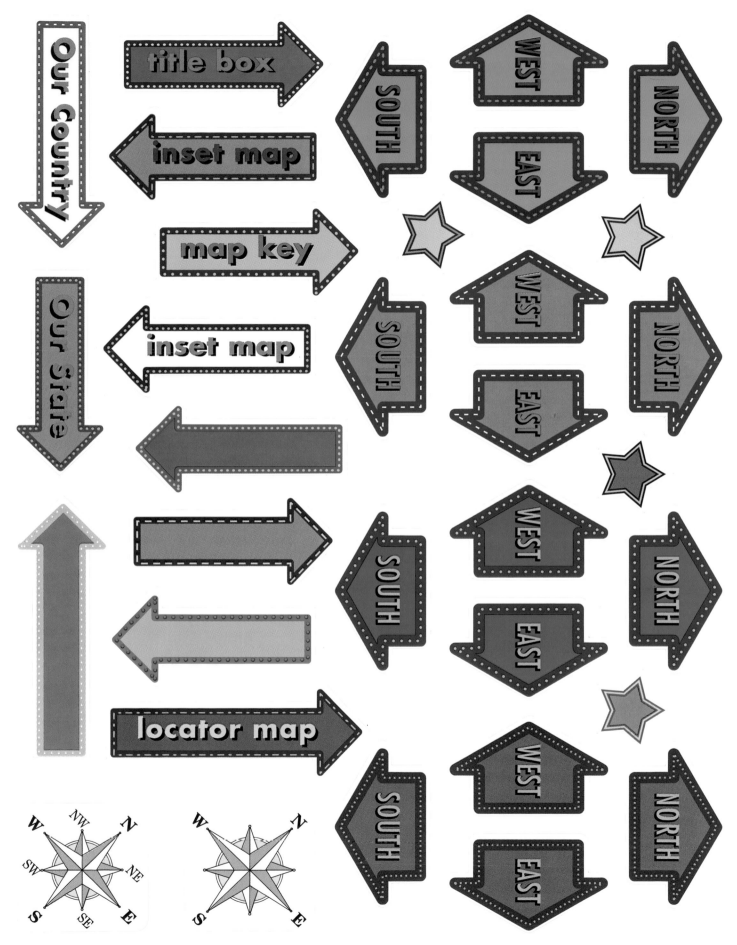

STICKER SHEET 2

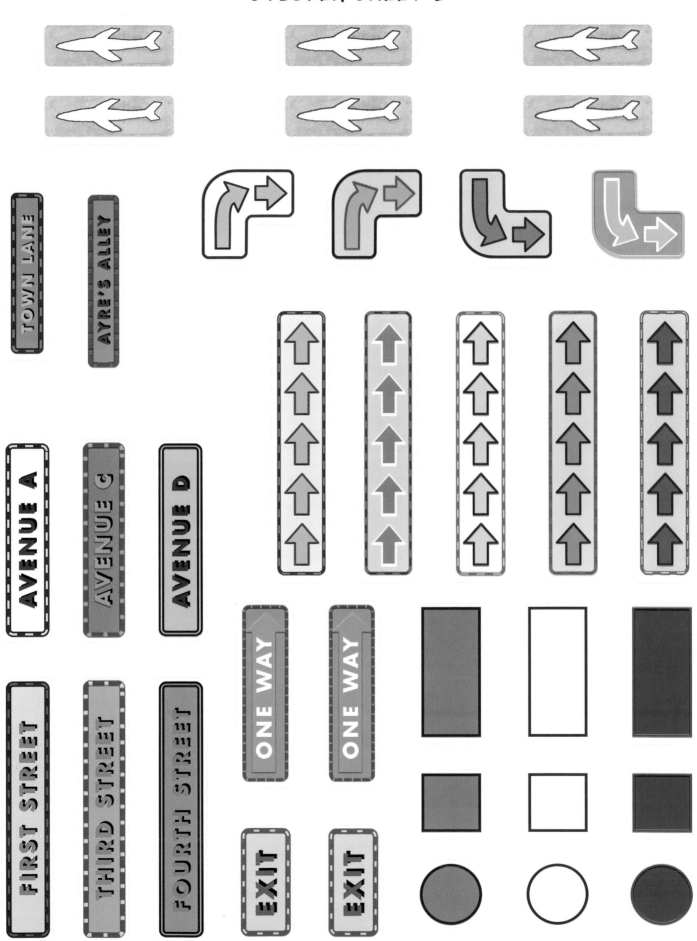

STICKER SHEET 3

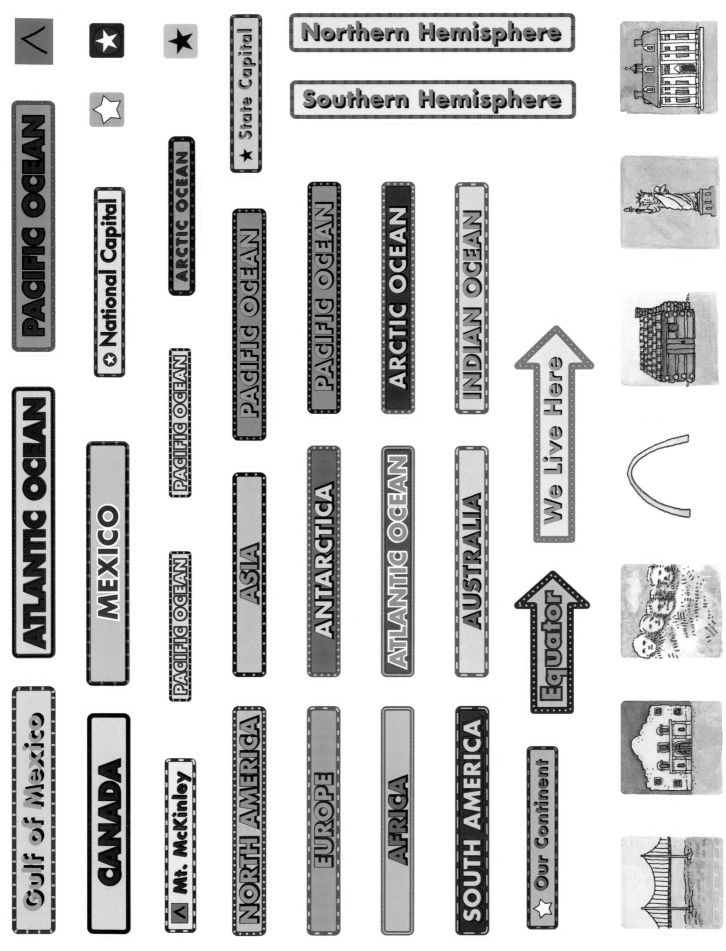

Pacific Ocean · National Capital · Arctic Ocean · State Capital

Northern Hemisphere

Southern Hemisphere

Atlantic Ocean · Mexico · Pacific Ocean · Pacific Ocean · Pacific Ocean · Arctic Ocean · Indian Ocean

Gulf of Mexico · Canada · Mt. McKinley · Pacific Ocean · Asia · Antarctica · Atlantic Ocean · Australia · We Live Here

North America · Europe · Africa · South America · Equator · Our Continent

STICKER SHEET 4

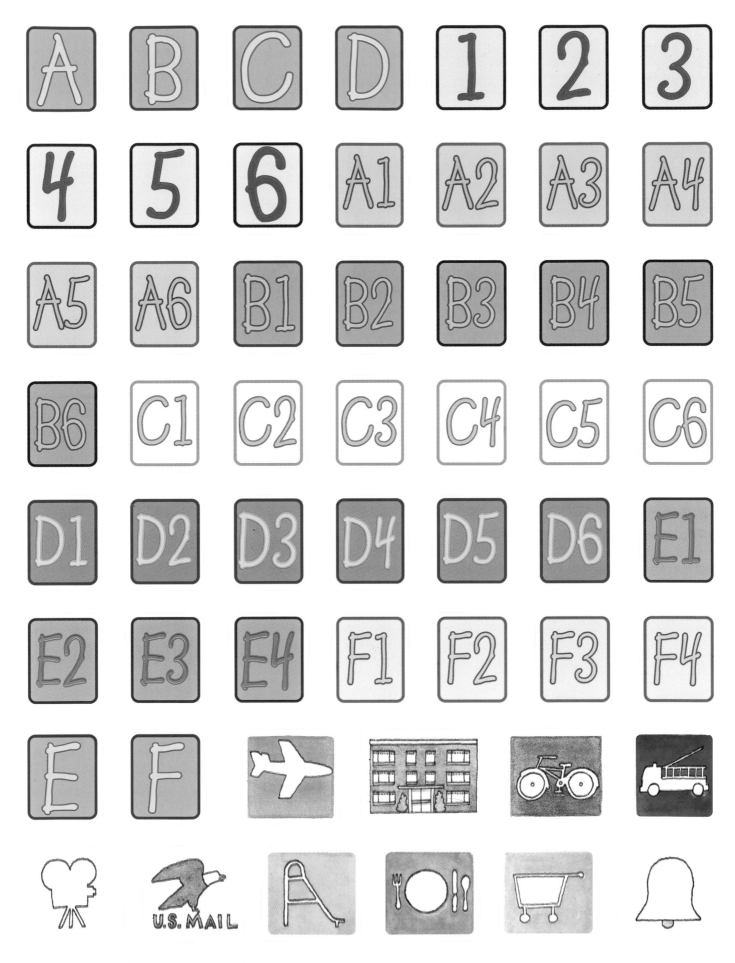

Name _____

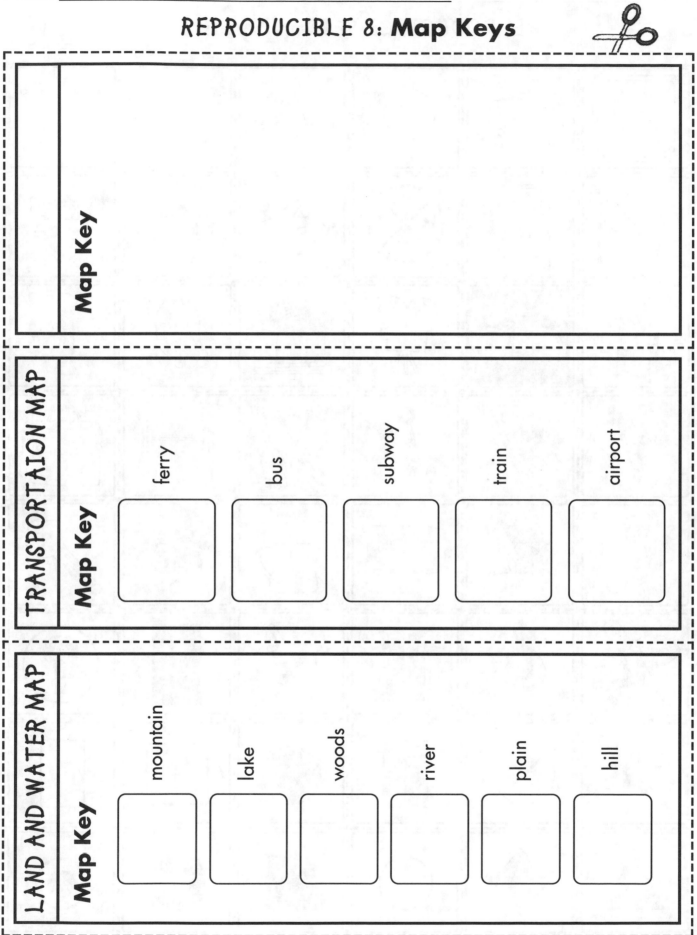

Map Key

TRANSPORTAION MAP

Map Key

ferry

bus

subway

train

airport

LAND AND WATER MAP

Map Key

mountain

lake

woods

river

plain

hill

REPRODUCIBLE 9: Map Symbols

MEGA-FUN MAP SKILLS
Scholastic Professional Books, 1999

REPRODUCIBLE 10: Map Symbols

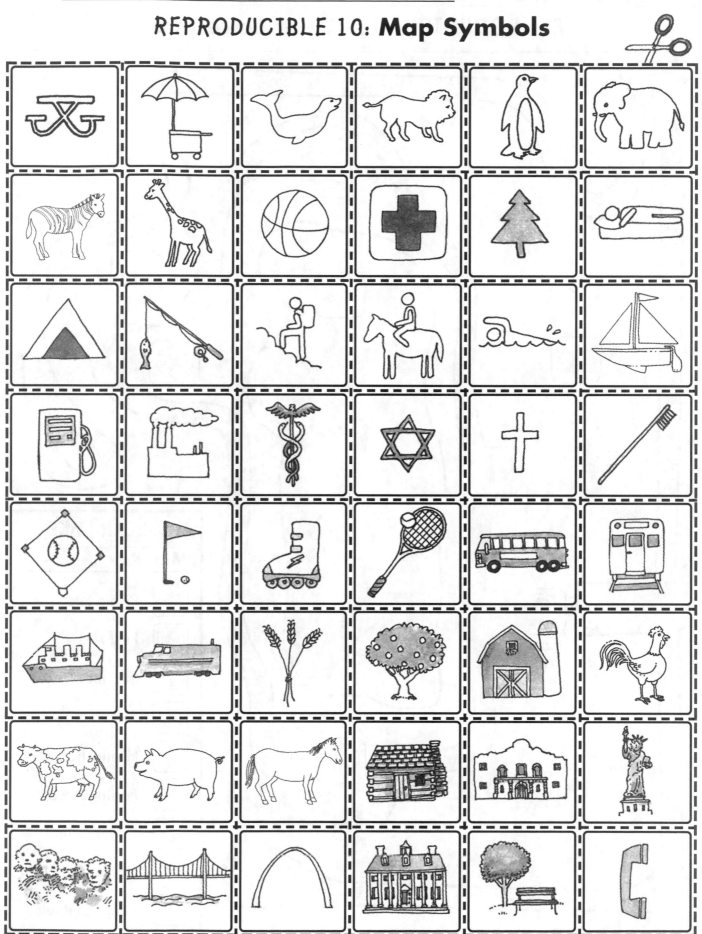

REPRODUCIBLE 11: Clear Lake Map

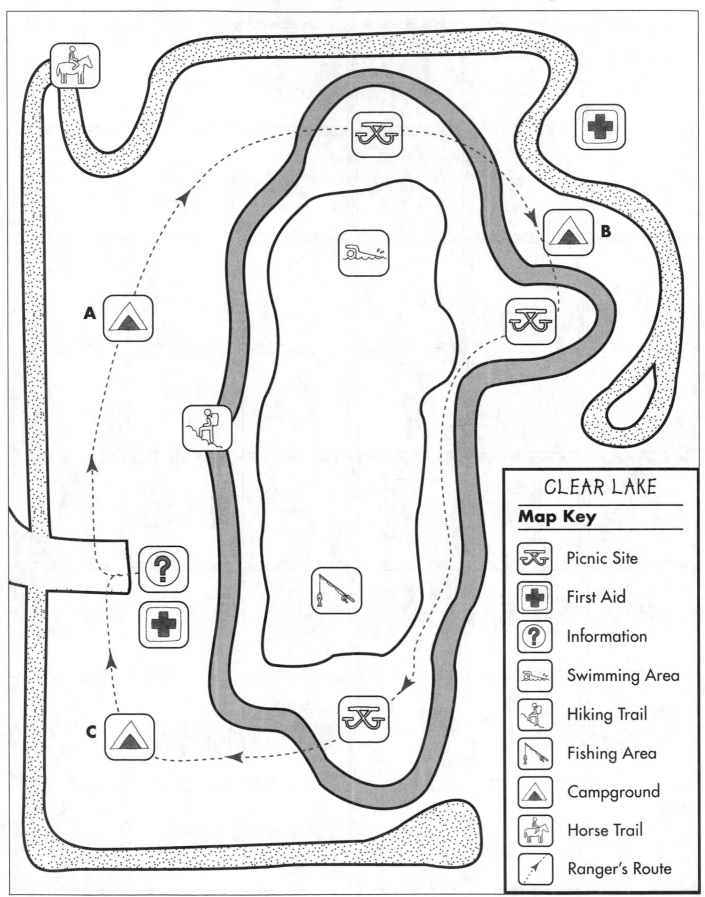

CLEAR LAKE

Map Key

⋊⋉	Picnic Site
✚	First Aid
?	Information
🏊	Swimming Area
🥾	Hiking Trail
🎣	Fishing Area
⛰	Campground
🏇	Horse Trail
↗	Ranger's Route

MEGA-FUN MAP SKILLS
Scholastic Professional Books, 1999

REPRODUCIBLE 12: **Earth's Directions Map**

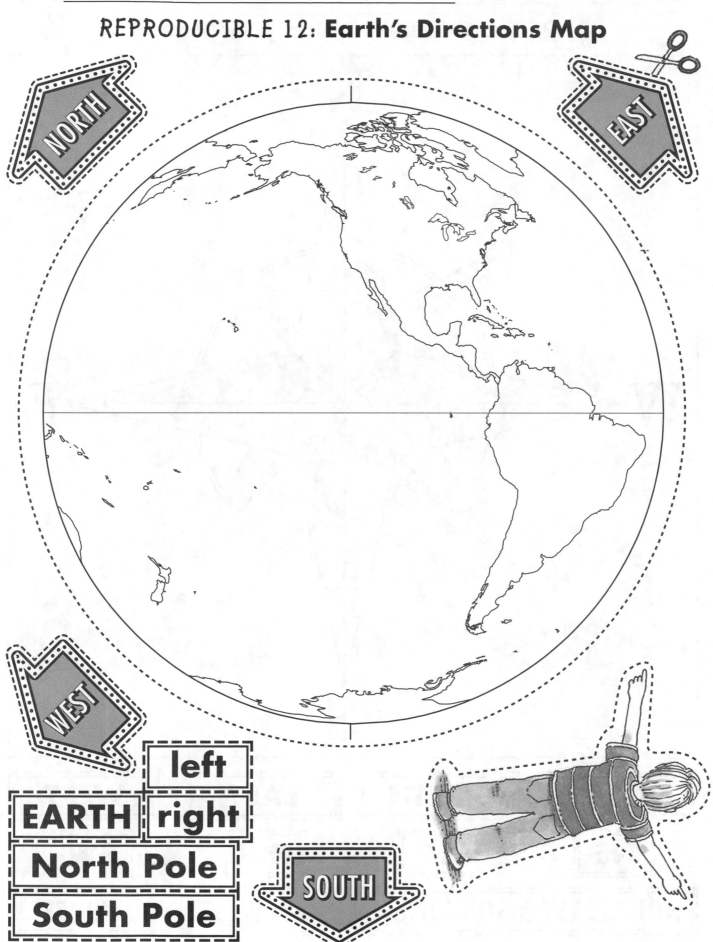

NORTH

EAST

WEST

SOUTH

left

EARTH   right

North Pole

South Pole

REPRODUCIBLE 13: **Compass Rose**

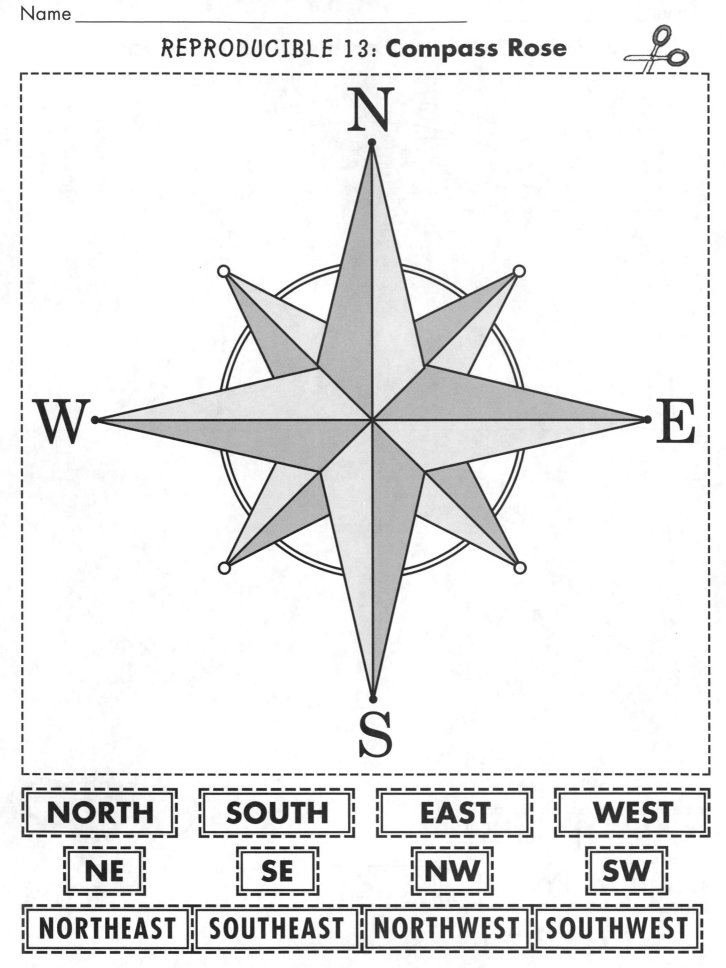

| NORTH | SOUTH | EAST | WEST |

| NE | SE | NW | SW |

| NORTHEAST | SOUTHEAST | NORTHWEST | SOUTHWEST |

MEGA-FUN MAP SKILLS
Scholastic Professional Books, 1999

REPRODUCIBLE 14: Play Land Floor Plan

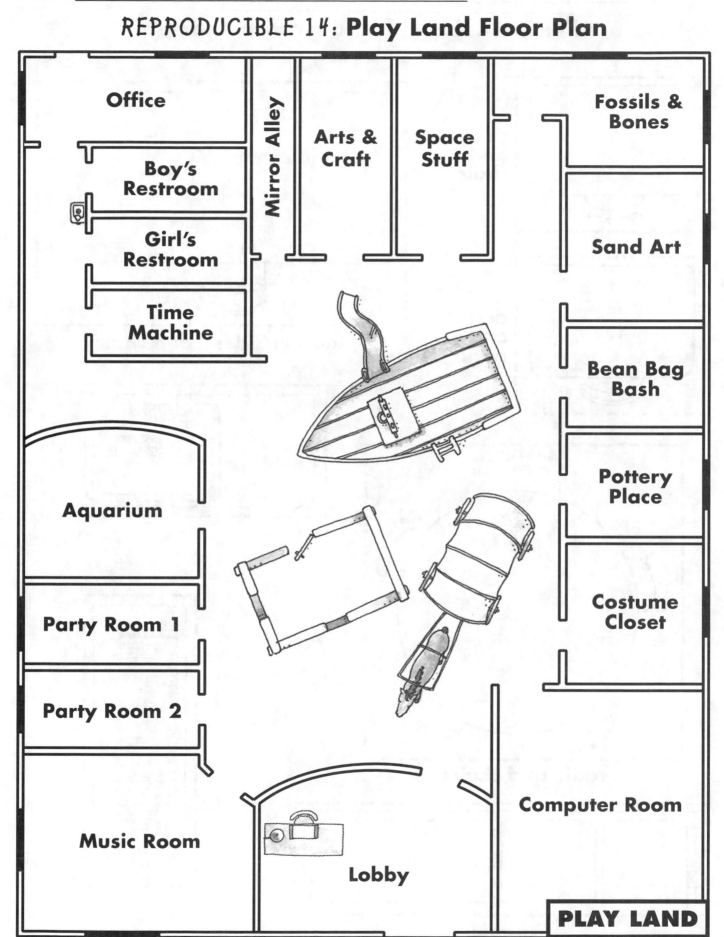

Office

Boy's Restroom

Girl's Restroom

Time Machine

Mirror Alley

Arts & Craft

Space Stuff

Fossils & Bones

Sand Art

Bean Bag Bash

Pottery Place

Costume Closet

Aquarium

Party Room 1

Party Room 2

Music Room

Lobby

Computer Room

PLAY LAND

REPRODUCIBLE 15: Classroom Cutouts

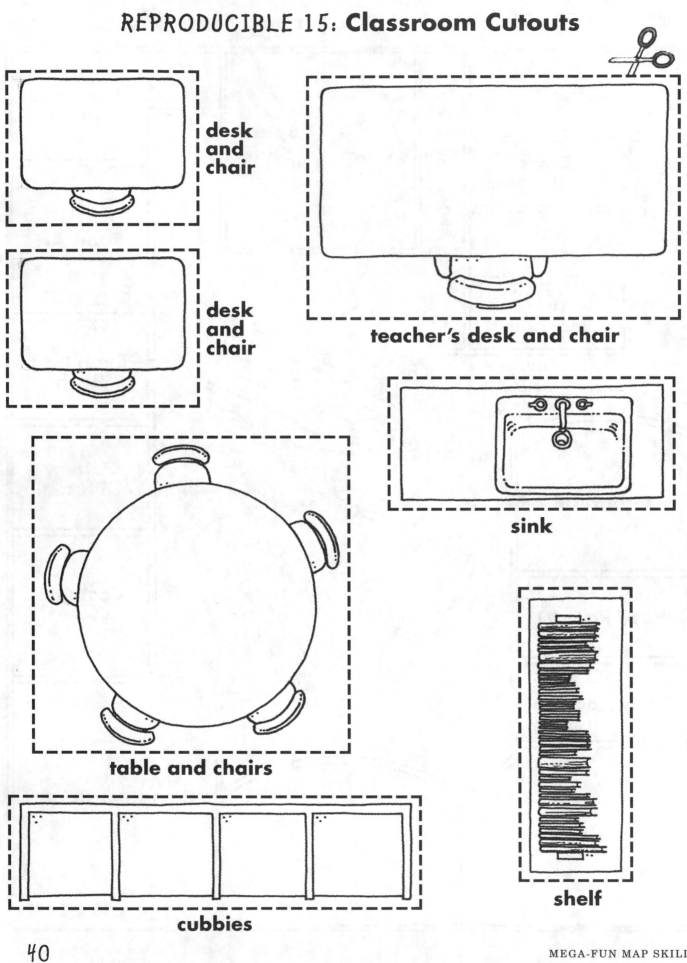

desk and chair

desk and chair

teacher's desk and chair

sink

table and chairs

shelf

cubbies

MEGA-FUN MAP SKILLS
Scholastic Professional Books, 1999

REPRODUCIBLE 16: **School Symbols**

REPRODUCIBLE 17: **Mall Floor Plan**

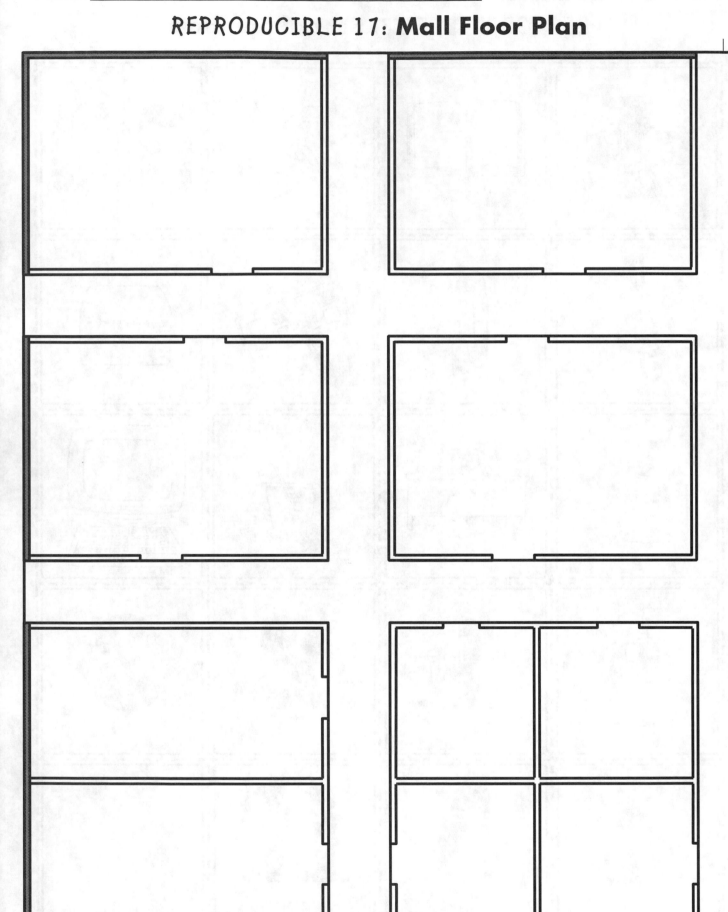

MEGA-FUN MAP SKILLS
Scholastic Professional Books, 1999

REPRODUCIBLE 18: **Mall Floor Plan**

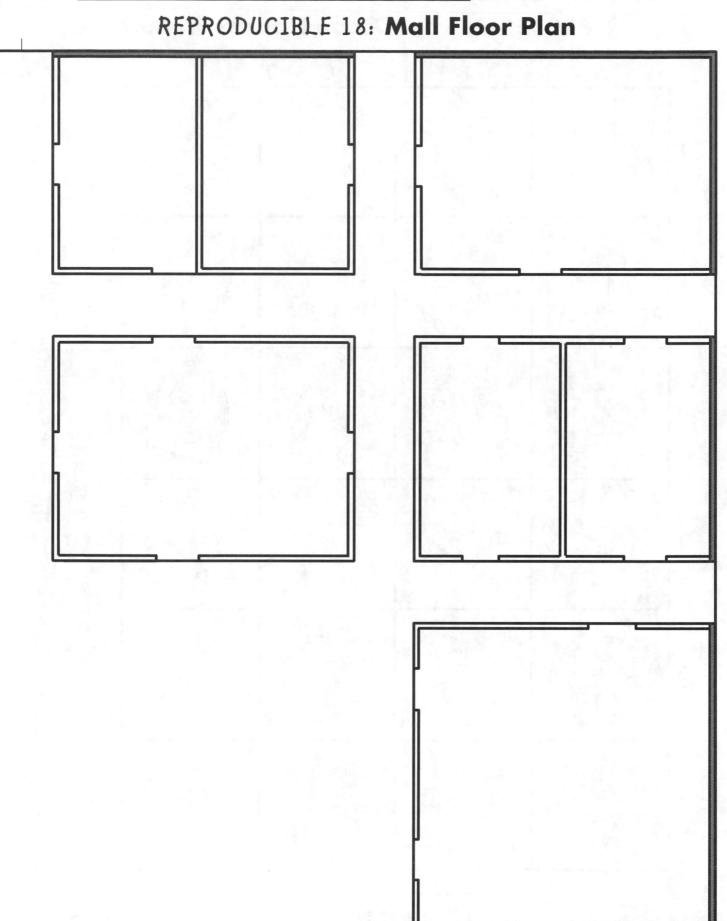

REPRODUCIBLE 19: Ocean Floor Grid Map

Ocean Treasure

MEGA-FUN MAP SKILLS
Scholastic Professional Books, 1999

REPRODUCIBLE 20: **Blank Grid Map**

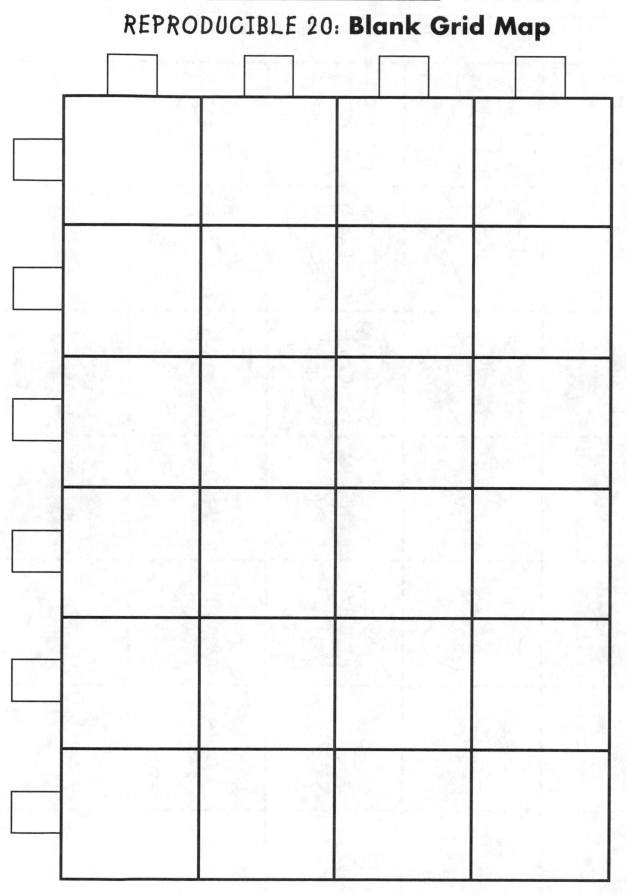

REPRODUCIBLE 21: **Garden Greens Cutouts**

MEGA-FUN MAP SKILLS
Scholastic Professional Books, 1999

REPRODUCIBLE 22: **Urban Area Map**

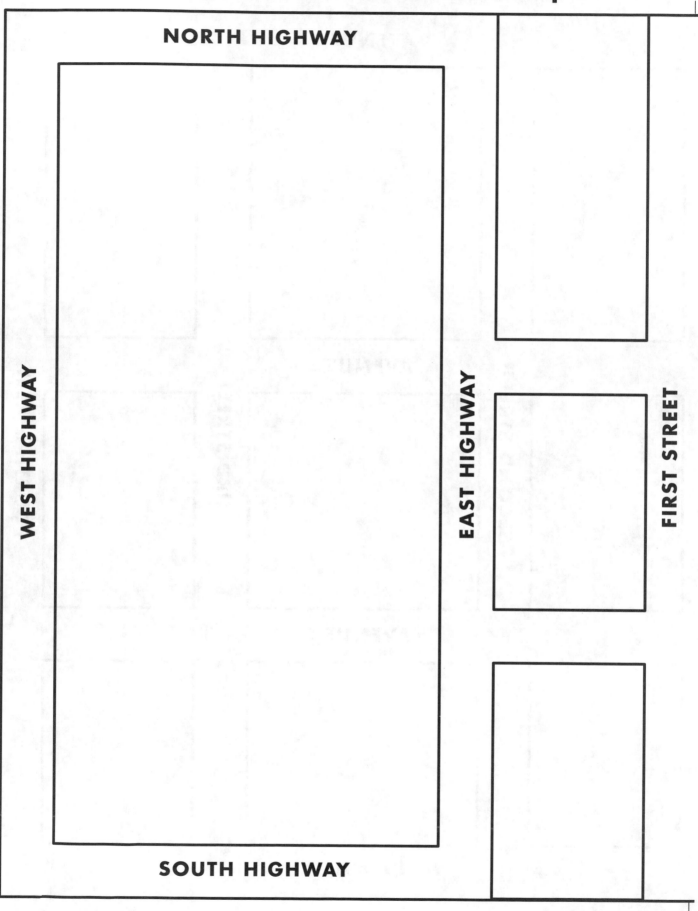

NORTH HIGHWAY

WEST HIGHWAY

EAST HIGHWAY

FIRST STREET

SOUTH HIGHWAY

REPRODUCIBLE 23: **Urban Area Map**

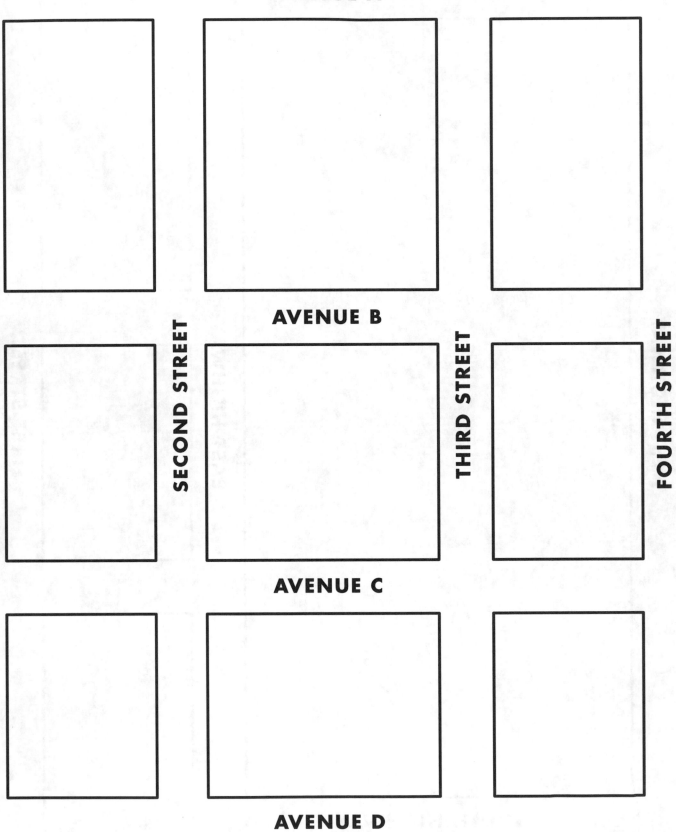

AVENUE A

AVENUE B

AVENUE C

AVENUE D

SECOND STREET

THIRD STREET

FOURTH STREET

Name _____

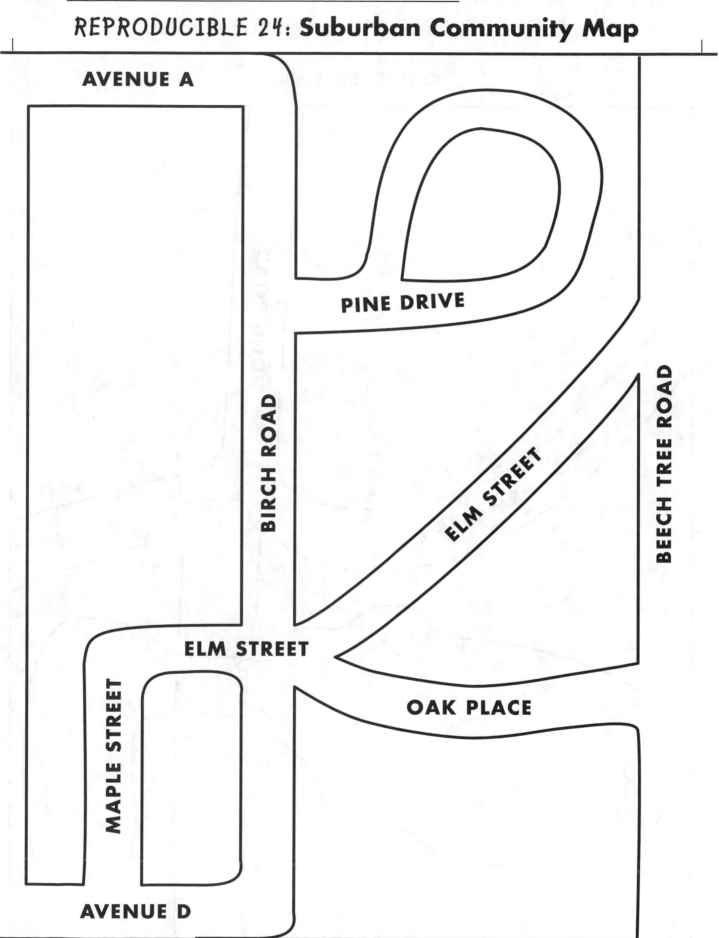

AVENUE A

PINE DRIVE

BIRCH ROAD

ELM STREET

BEECH TREE ROAD

ELM STREET

MAPLE STREET

OAK PLACE

AVENUE D

REPRODUCIBLE 25: **Rural Area Map**

ORCHARD LANE

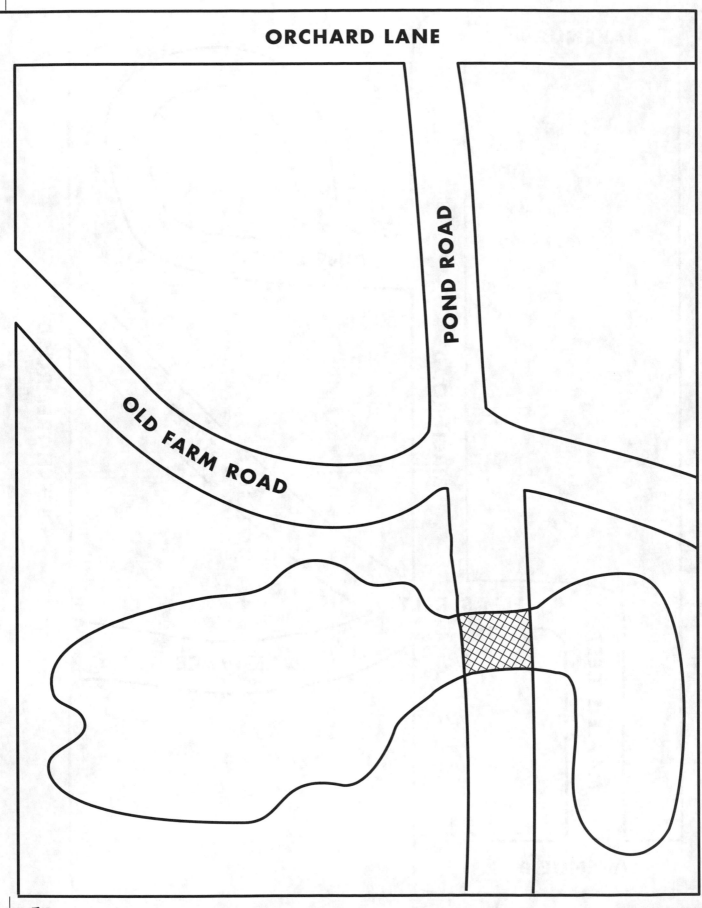

POND ROAD

OLD FARM ROAD

MEGA-FUN MAP SKILLS
Scholastic Professional Books, 1999

REPRODUCIBLE 26: Transportation Map

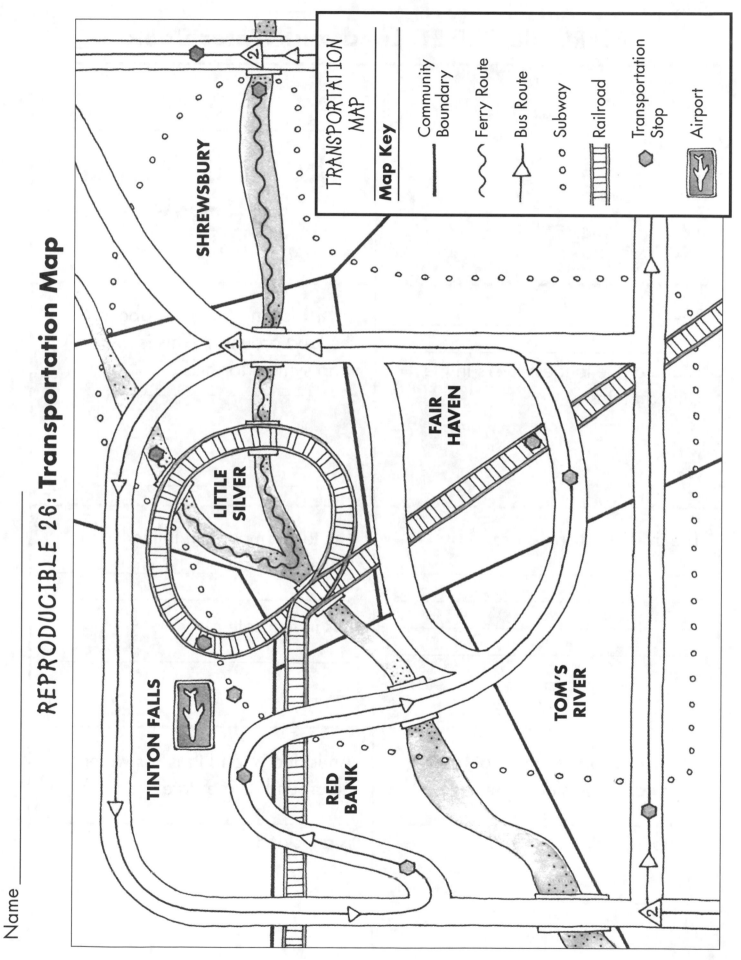

REPRODUCIBLE 27: Land and Water Book

_____'s

Land & Water Book

The _____
_____
is one of the longest rivers in the
United States.

13

A **hill** is land that rises above
the land around it. This is my
map symbol for hills.

2

The five Great Lakes are

_____

_____

_____

and _____ .

11

The tallest mountain in the
United States is _____
_____.

It is in the state of
_____.

4

A **peninsula** is land that has
water on three sides. The state
of _____
is a peninsula.

9

An island is land that has water
all around it. The state of
_____
is an island.

6

52

fold

MEGA-FUN MAP SKILLS
Scholastic Professional Books, 1999

REPRODUCIBLE 28: Land and Water Book

A **plain** is very flat land. This is my map symbol for plains.

1

An **ocean** is a very large body of salt water. Three oceans that border the United States are the

_____

_____

and _____.

Mountains are the highest kind of land. This is my map symbol for mountains.

3

A **river** is a long body of water that flows across the land. This is my symbol for a river.

12

A **desert** is a dry place with very little rain. This is my map symbol for desert.

5

A **lake** is a body of water with land all around it. This is my picture symbol for a lake.

10

A **valley** is low lands between hills or mountains. A **canyon** is a very, very deep valley.

7

A famous canyon in the United States is the _____

_____

It is in the state of

_____.

8

Name _____

_____

MAP KEY

54

Name_____

REPRODUCIBLE 30: **United States Map**

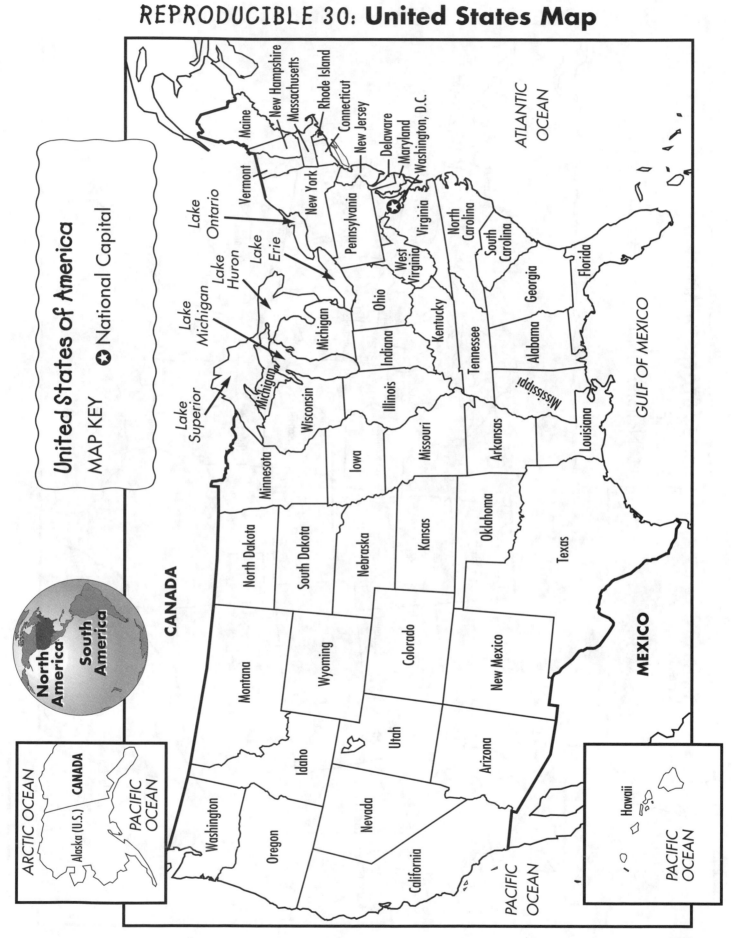

REPRODUCIBLE 31: **United States Capital Cities**

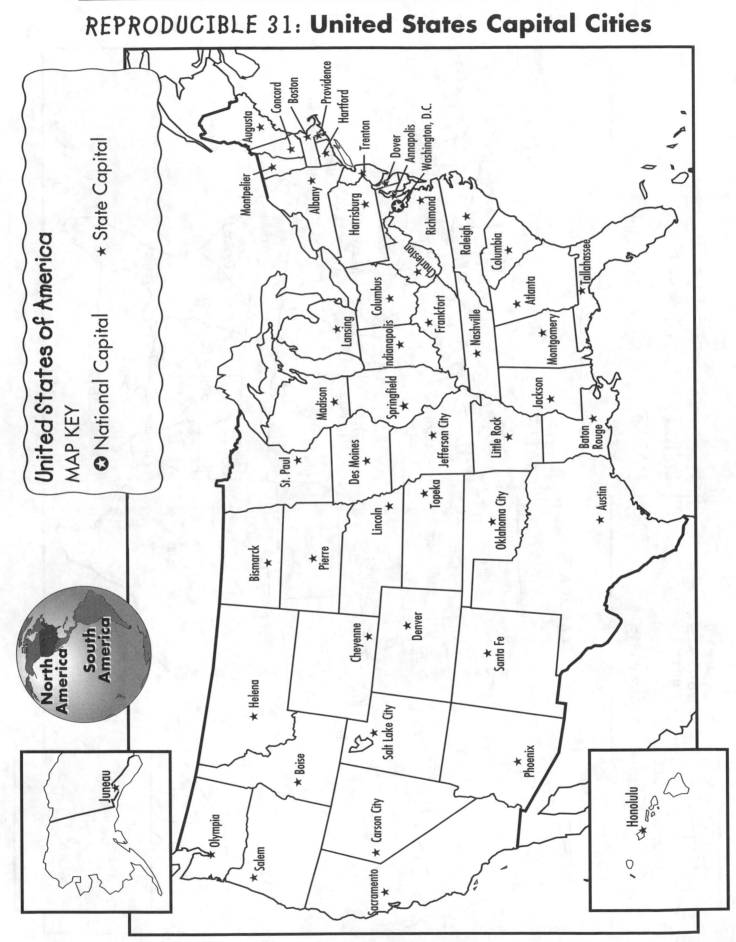

United States of America
MAP KEY

⊕ National Capital   ★ State Capital

North America

South America

Augusta ★

Concord
Boston
Providence
Hartford

Montpelier

Trenton
Dover
Annapolis
Washington, D.C.

Albany ★

Harrisburg

Richmond ★

Charleston

Raleigh ★

Columbia ★

Columbus ★

Frankfort ★

Atlanta ★

Tallahassee ★

Lansing ★

Indianapolis ★

Nashville ★

Montgomery ★

Madison ★

Springfield ★

Jackson ★

St. Paul ★

Des Moines ★

Jefferson City ★

Little Rock ★

Baton Rouge ★

Topeka ★

Lincoln ★

Oklahoma City ★

Austin ★

Bismarck ★

Pierre ★

Cheyenne ★

Denver ★

Santa Fe ★

Helena ★

Salt Lake City ★

Phoenix ★

Boise ★

Carson City ★

Honolulu ★

Juneau ★

Olympia ★

Salem ★

Sacramento ★

56

Name _____

REPRODUCIBLE 32: **North America Map**

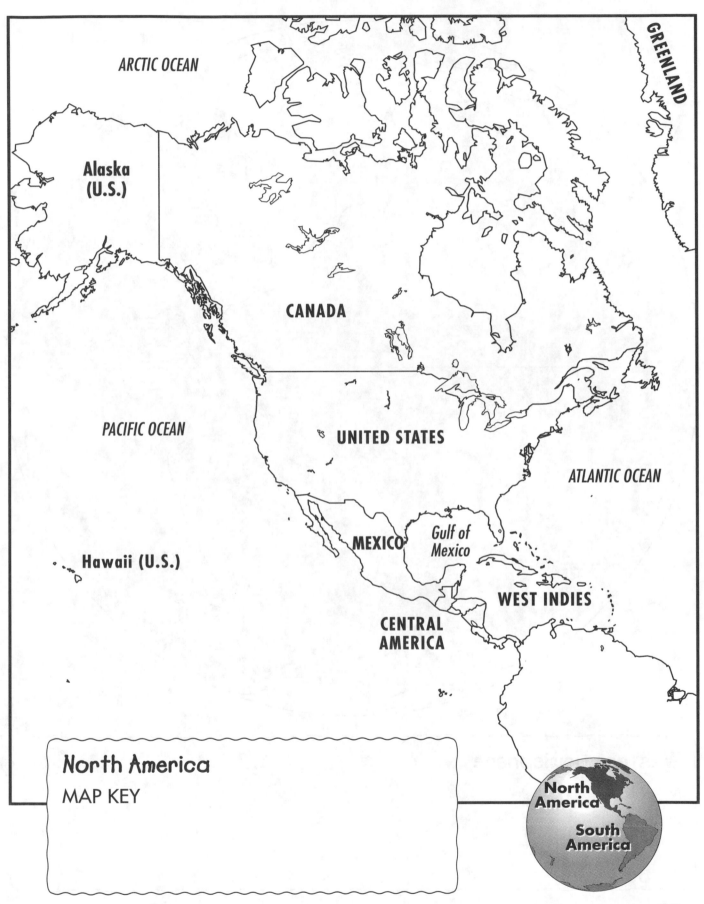

ARCTIC OCEAN

GREENLAND

Alaska
(U.S.)

CANADA

PACIFIC OCEAN

UNITED STATES

ATLANTIC OCEAN

Hawaii (U.S.)

MEXICO

Gulf of
Mexico

WEST INDIES

CENTRAL
AMERICA

North America

MAP KEY

North
America

South
America

REPRODUCIBLE 33: **Western Hemisphere Map**

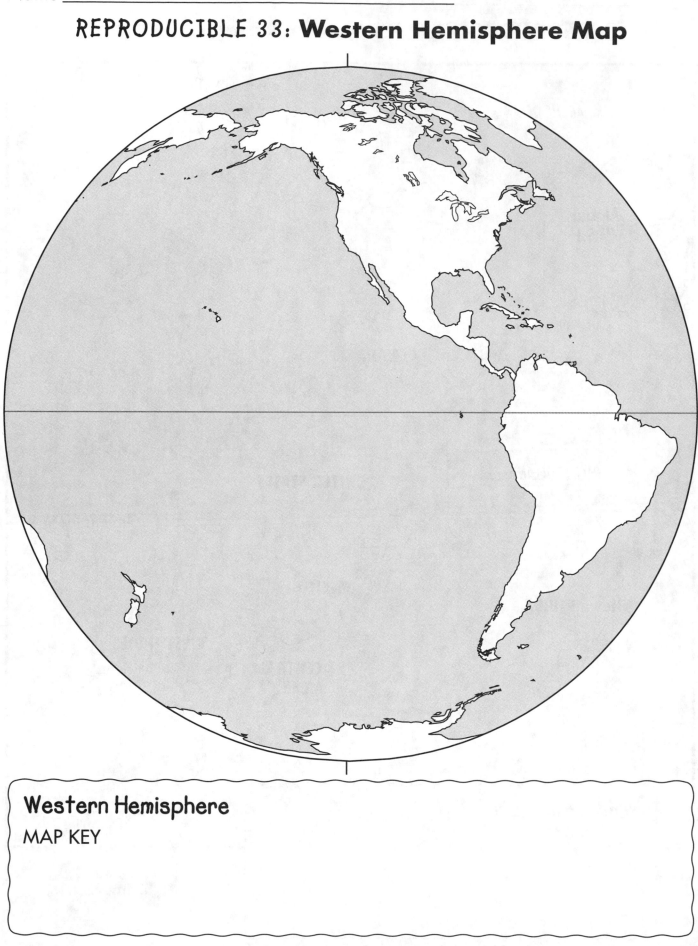

Western Hemisphere

MAP KEY

MEGA-FUN MAP SKILLS
Scholastic Professional Books, 1999

Name _____

REPRODUCIBLE 34: **Eastern Hemisphere Map**

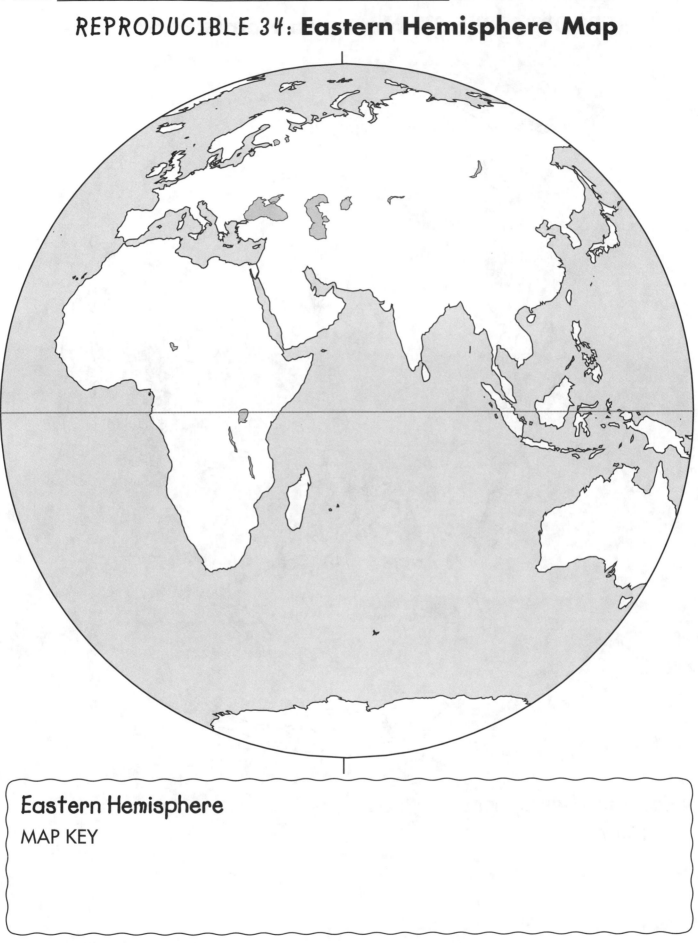

Eastern Hemisphere

MAP KEY

REPRODUCIBLE 35: **Northern Hemisphere Map**

Northern Hemisphere

MAP KEY

MEGA-FUN MAP SKILLS
Scholastic Professional Books, 1999

REPRODUCIBLE 36: **Southern Hemisphere Map**

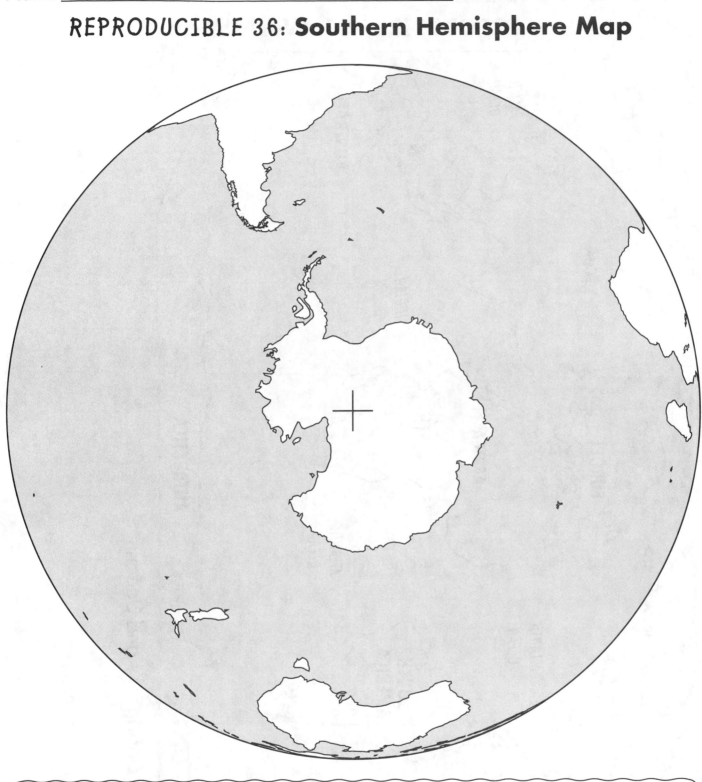

Southern Hemisphere

MAP KEY

REPRODUCIBLE 37: **World Map**

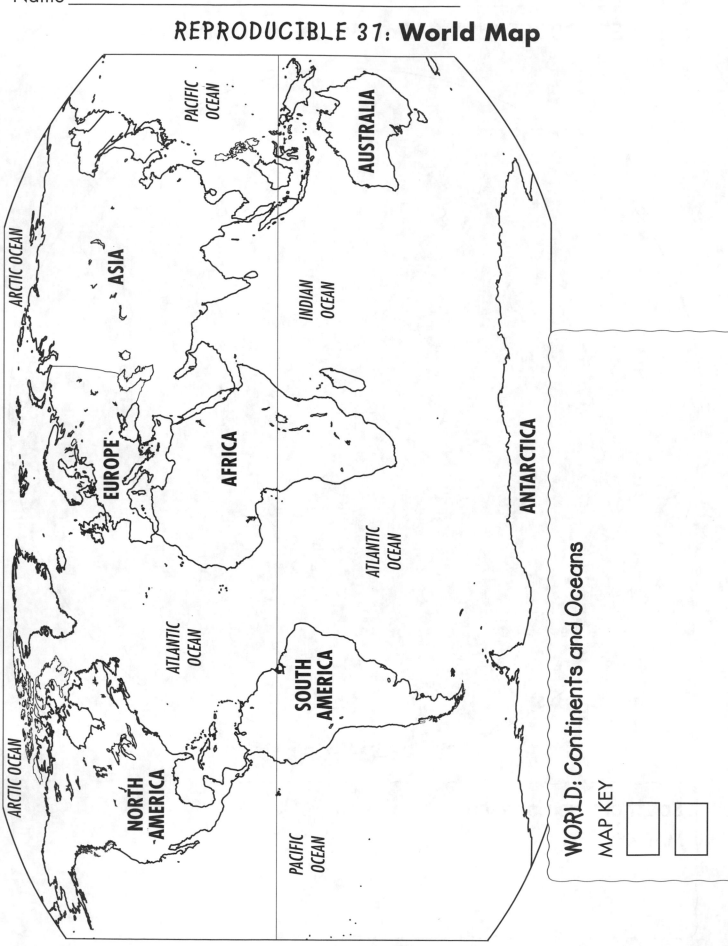

PACIFIC OCEAN

AUSTRALIA

ARCTIC OCEAN

ASIA

INDIAN OCEAN

EUROPE

AFRICA

ANTARCTICA

ATLANTIC OCEAN

ATLANTIC OCEAN

SOUTH AMERICA

ARCTIC OCEAN

NORTH AMERICA

PACIFIC OCEAN

WORLD: Continents and Oceans

MAP KEY

MEGA-FUN MAP SKILLS
Scholastic Professional Books, 1999

Notes